Y'all Come Over

DEDICATION

For my grandmother, Sarah Dopson, and all of the Southern women who
have passed down the art of Southern etiquette and the love of hospitality.
Parties of today are a result of the legacy you all leave.

Y'all Come Over
Charming Your Guests with New Recipes, Heirloom Treasures,
and True Southern Hospitality
by Rebecca Lang

First published in 2021 in the United States of America by
Rizzoli International Publications, Inc.
300 Park Avenue South
New York, NY 10010
rizzoliusa.com

© 2021 by Rebecca Lang
rebeccalangcooks.com

Publisher: Charles Miers
Editor: Jono Jarrett
Design: Teresa Cole
Production Manager: Colin Hough-Trapp
Managing Editor: Lynn Scrabis

Printed in China
2021 2022 2023 2024 / 10 9 8 7 6 5 4 3 2 1

ISBN: ISBN 978-0-7893-3771-9
Library of Congress Call Number: 2021934007

Pages 1, 12, 13, 15, 16, 18, 21, 31, 39, 47, 49, 50, 52, 56, 59, 71, 81, 82, 83,
86-87, 91, 97, 98, 102-103, 121, 132, 138, 231, and 238:
Photography by Kathryn McCrary
kathrynmccrary.com

Pages 83 and 138: Illustrations by Adair Lang

Prop styling by Missie Crawford
missieneville crawford.com

Visit us online:
Facebook.com/RizzoliNewYork
Twitter: @Rizzoli_Books
Instagram.com/RizzoliBooks
Pinterest.com/RizzoliBooks
Youtube.com/user/RizzoliNY

Y'all Come Over

Charming Your Guests with New Recipes, Heirloom Treasures, and True Southern Hospitality

Rizzoli

New York Paris London Milan

REBECCA LANG

Contents

1

Introduction

It's always time to have a party! Once you host one
gathering, you are almost guaranteed to host your second.
Letting all the fun of welcoming others into your house pass
you by until you have the perfect set of plates is simply wasting
precious time. Send out an invitation and open the door to
friends and family. You'll soon find you are the only
one that even notices anything less than perfect.

Southern Hospitality

Throwing a noteworthy party in the South takes more than just cooking and inviting friends over. A memorable gathering, no matter the size or occasion, is a clear reflection of genuine hospitality and how it's shown in your home in every detail. Each guest who walks in the door should be treated to an experience of utmost comfort and ease. From visiting with neighbors, to hosting a crowd, to pulling cheese straws out of the freezer when a friend drives up, this authentic culture of comfort is universal in the South and very much in effect all over the region. And of course, you don't have to born in the South to have the gift of hospitality. It's simply a result of thoughtfulness and graciousness, which are not tied to your hometown's location on a map.

Simply put, being a good host means thinking ahead to anticipate the needs of guests in your home. Proper etiquette and manners should be your guide. Think of etiquette as the code of conduct, while manners operate within the rules of etiquette. These are two of the keys to successful life in the South and will always be a part of hospitality at home no matter where you live. Virginia Johnson's Contemporary School of Etiquette in Houston, Texas, explains it well: "Etiquette is a set of rules, but good manners are from the heart."

Being hospitable and having good etiquette is an organic combination, and it's a combination that always opens the door to the best gatherings. One does not exist without the other. While not everyone in the South is well mannered, most of us, including my children, learned the art of "yes, ma'am" before they could write. These skills are certainly valuable for hosts, as the ability to throw a terrific Southern party depends on etiquette. It is not an extra, not icing on the cake—it is essential. And often, when an adult has less than ideal manners, it's blamed on his or her mother for failing to teach the fundamentals. Each time I take my son to cotillion class, I'm hoping that blame won't ever fall on me.

Ask someone who's not from around here what people in the South are like and it's likely you'll hear a comment about our good manners and our rich food. Men hold open doors, everyone waves to each other on the road, and the ma'ams are abundant. It's true, things are different.

y'all Come Over!

Y ou can never say that phrase too often. It's an instant invitation for two friends, a large crowd, or anything in between. Hosting others in your home is one of the most sincere forms of generosity and warmth, and this simple combination of words lets friends know they are valued and welcome. Just as a recipe teaches the steps of making a dish that you want to cook, these pages will give you all the tools you need to open your front door with confidence and charm.

Southern etiquette is the defining element that separates average gatherings from unforgettable events. Parties in the South are comfortable, without intimidation, and are milestones that hosts look forward to and approach almost stress free—if you're not one of these hosts, don't worry, this book will help get you there!

Southern hospitality can be acquired and mastered to create parties that are more organized and more thoughtful. Tips and tricks are in the pages to come to make every guest that walks in the door feel comfortable and wanted every moment in your home. Acquire these Southern secrets of entertaining by learning the art of etiquette in each area of your home. A great party starts by planning at the desk and ends when you turn on the dishwasher.

Learn to plan ahead and check off tasks to make things easier on the day of the party. You'll find you can't wait for that first ring of the doorbell. The last-minute flight-of-the-bumblebee party prep won't be needed anymore. Stocking the bar is easy with guidance on exactly what you want to drink. Cooking recipes to impress is done mostly ahead and completed on time. Even your home is clean and ready for guests. With the finesse created from a little Southern hospitality, anyone anywhere can host their friends and enjoy every single second of it. Never before has opening the door to guests been more treasured. A craving for company, face to face, over a glass of something festive and a comforting plate can come close to the desire for water or air. No matter the size of your home or your budget, entertaining can be a sparkling light in your life. Making room to welcome others is a blessing that spills onto everyone invited.

> "Southern etiquette is the defining element that separates average gatherings from unforgettable events."

Jump Right in

Becoming a wonderful host can't happen until you host your first party. If entertaining has always been something you want to do—do it! It's too fun to put off until you feel more confident, have new furniture, or that fresh coat of paint you've been thinking about.

One of the easiest ways to entertain for the very first time is to host a party before a party. When a group of friends plan to attend a holiday party, spring soirée, or a big tailgate on campus, invite them over to your house first. If everyone is on the way to a larger event, a pre-party party becomes an easy and inexpensive way to begin a lifetime of successful entertaining.

Make sure that each person invited to your home is also attending the party later on. Unlike other parties, this type of impromptu gathering can be short, even 45 minutes, and just require a very basic bar offering and a nibble or two to snack on. Unlike hosting other events, it's completely fine (even necessary) to remind guests of the time so all of you can be on time for the main event.

Etiquette in Today's Lifestyle

Each year life seems to get busier and more hectic. We are surrounded by screens, and pen and paper seem in short supply in many homes. Even with these changes, etiquette is still imperative and remains steady in its importance, perhaps even more so. The more intensely and quickly that real life happens, the more we have a need for moments of genuine hospitality. Don't let the excuse of living in a fast-paced world overcome one of the very best things about the South. When your friends hear, "Y'all come over," the swirl of to-do lists and obligations seems to slow down and so the congregating can begin.

Etiquette 101: Becoming Perfectly Polished

Southern finishing schools and cotillion classes led the way in Southern etiquette for generations and have helped to keep it alive. Luckily, there's a school in our hometown of Athens, Georgia, and we take advantage of every instruction. Our son, Camden, and almost every other middle school child we know takes etiquette classes from Debra Lassiter at her school, Perfectly Polished. I'm convinced our town is more refined because of her efforts.

As these types of graceful, charming sessions are becoming less commonly taught, it's important to look back on some of the most vital lessons, which are applicable if you are a host or a guest. Please refresh, if needed:

⇒ Always look a person in the eye when talking and give them your full attention.

⇒ Graciously accept a compliment with a thank-you and a smile.

⇒ Write timely, hand-written thank-you notes.

⇒ Make good conversation, even with people you don't know.

⇒ Hosting others in your home is a way of showing that you value the relationship.

⇒ Arrive on time.

⇒ Treat others the way you would like to be treated.

Small Budgets

Successful parties are possible when budgets are small; here's what you can do:

Send free e-invitations. • Save the vases when you get flowers from a florist—they are perfect to hold silverware on a buffet. • You don't need a lot of fancy china or glasses to have fun. Use what you have and buy an inexpensive, interesting accent platter or serving piece to liven up things. • Use random glasses (after the others in the set were lost long ago or broken) to hold garnishes on the bar or fill with little snacks. • Look for sales on linens and all things tabletop at your favorite discount home stores. • Clip flowers from your yard or window boxes for bud vases. • Make a punch or sangria to stretch the alcohol to serve more guests for less cost.

Entertaining on a Real-Life Budget

Entertaining can be expensive—sometimes really expensive—but it doesn't have to be. If you wait to entertain until you can afford the most elaborate party, you're missing out on all the fun. You'll find tips throughout this book for hosting memorable gatherings on a budget, but in a nutshell: It requires thinking ahead and relaxing. Your guests aren't concerned about how much you spend, so don't get hung up on that either. Never apologize for what you have or don't have. Be proud of your possessions and the food you serve. Embrace what you have and make it work!

Winning at Thoughtfulness
When Time is Short

We're all busy, so use these strategies for good
manners to be both a gracious host and a beloved
guest, even on the most harried of days:

⇒ Keep a pantry stash of staples that can become appetizers
in a flash for last-minute guests or offerings to a host.

⇒ When you have a free day on a weekend, cook and freeze
so your next party is already ahead of schedule.

⇒ After using any special-occasion items, wash and
put them away so they're ready for next time.

⇒ Buy fun paper cocktail napkins when you see them
on sale. You'll always use them.

⇒ Always, always RSVP (see page 24). In a pinch,
text your RSVP. The need to RSVP is what is set in
stone, not the method.

⇒ Have stamped envelopes with preprinted return addresses
ready at all times. Keep them in your purse, briefcase, or
carry-on for a quick note to be written when you have a
few minutes of downtime anywhere you go.

⇒ Buy hostess gifts in bulk and add a ribbon to be
gifted on a moment's notice.

⇒ Be courteous and smile. It doesn't take any time.

⇒ Try leaving your phone in the car when
attending a party. You'll save time by not
checking it and you'll actually be
present for the entire event.

My Favorite Southern Etiquette

I t's true that almost all things are different in the South. While some of the niceties I love the most about where I live ring true in other places, these really make living here a little sweeter. It's not that Southerners have more time than other people, I think we simply make time to be extra courteous. A few hospitable seconds can make a difference in amazing ways. Making a point to be thoughtful and nice to each other is always appreciated.

Always Wave

Southerners tend to wave more often than not. Standing in your yard, driving down the road, or seeing a someone you might recognize on the other side of the grocery store all deserve a wave. While growing up, I learned a rule to waving that applies mostly to when your hands are on the steering wheel. The more fingers that are raised in the wave, the better you know the recipient of the wave.

Opening and Holding the Door

I appreciate when anyone opens the door for me and always say thank you when they do. I still am in the belief that men should open doors for women and everyone should open the door for the elderly.

If ever I open a door in a public location, I turn to see if I need to hold the door open for someone coming close behind me. I am in the process of teaching my children to remember to do the same. It's the little things like this that really make a difference to total strangers that are busy running errands too.

Hand-written Recipe Cards

The Southern tradition of passing down handwritten recipes keeps family favorites alive for generations. My grandmother Sarah often wrote on any paper that was nearby. Many recipes in her kitchen were inscribed on the backs of clothing tags brought to her by her sister, Harriett. The "imperfect" tags had been used to designate flawed pants made at Roydon Wear, the local clothing manufacturing plant in my hometown of McRae, GA.

1/4 TEASPOON

1/2 TEASPOON

IMPERFE

Rejected Due to
___ Mill Flaw
___ Manufacturing Error
___ Shaded Spots

Place all (X) at location of imperfection
Water ___ Oil ___

FRONT BACK

RIGHT LEFT LEFT RIGHT

Southern Funeral Processions

Mourners follow the hearse from the church to the cemetery in an organized procession with each car shining headlights to indicate it is a part of the group. From the moment the line pulls out of the church, passing cars pull to the side of the road and wait until the line has passed. When cars begin to come without their headlights on, other drivers know it's okay to continue down the road. Red lights are held by local police as family and friends drive slowly to their loved one's final resting place. If you have ever lost someone you loved and buried them in the South, you know the meaning of these thoughtful and respectful gestures.

Casseroles in the Car

Southern women can drive a casserole nearly anywhere in town and keep it hot and ready for serving. Occasions that need food like a death, a birth, a sickness, or anything in between practically require a casserole. There are all kinds of unique ways of transporting a 13 x 9 dish in backseats and floorboards. Layers of foil with old (but clean) bath towels wrapped around each dish is a good one. Scraps of rug pads placed under layers of kitchen towels and topped with a hot Pyrex works well. But my favorite is one that I've seen my mom do countless times. My dad will drive with the utmost of care with a top speed of 20 mph while my mom sits in the passenger side with her legs completely still. In her lap is a thick tray topped with hot pads that have seen better days, then a steaming hot casserole covered in foil and a kitchen towel laid on top.

Ma'ams and Sirs

I forget how common and lovely a yes ma'am is to hear until I travel north or west and those words become few and far between. Using those tiny phrases to anyone that is older than you or to anyone who is helping you in any capacity is a display of respect.

Welcoming Neighbors

When Southerners see a moving van, hot food is normally not far behind. Bringing a gift of food to the door serves a couple of purposes. Providing food can make the first few days in a new home a little easier. Ringing the doorbell with food in hand also makes a great ice-breaker to meeting the new additions to the neighborhood.

Notes for No Reason

Receiving a thank-you note is always a bright spot in the day but opening a note sent for no reason is like sunshine. Southerners write notes sometimes for just a thought or a memory they enjoy or just to say hello. A mailbox should never be empty.

Sit on the Porch

If sitting on the porch was a sport, I'm pretty sure the championship would always be here in the South. Southerners first took a liking to the porch to be cooler before the days of air-conditioning. Now we like it so we can see neighbors walking by and listen to cicadas in the summer. And, thank goodness many porches now have ceiling fans.

YOU'RE INVITED

WHAT
brunch

WHEN
sunday noon

WHERE
rebecca's porch

RSVP
404-
637-
1223

2

At the Desk

A few minutes of planning smooths the way for the best get-togethers. Long before any groceries are bought or pillows are fluffed, the makings of a great party start at the desk. Writing a realistic plan first and foremost will make your life easier, I promise. This is the quiet time where you can think of the best time of day that works for your celebration and who should be invited. You can decide what menu would work for your schedule and just what should the invitation say. Planning is probably the easiest step of hosting friends, but one that is just as important as any other.

Invitations

A party begins with the invitations, so start the party planning off in a timely fashion by sending them out with an appropriate lead time. The general rule is that the more formal the party, the earlier the invitations need to go out. Also, guests usually appreciate an earlier invite during especially busy times of year, like December and June. Four weeks is a good guideline for formal dinner parties, bridal gatherings, and baby showers. For more casual events, two to three weeks is ideal. Remember if you are mailing the invitations, make sure there's time for delivery. No matter what method you choose to invite your guests, the solid rule is that all guests are invited in the same manner.

The Joys of Paper

We now live in a time when the mailman is rarely the method of delivery for invitations. For that reason, I adore paper invitations. When an invitation arrives in the mailbox it shows thoughtfulness, time, and planning, and it feels like a little gift for anyone who is on the guest list. Paper also seems to give the party an instant feeling of priority and importance. I've learned from experience that snafus in the post office can occur. Send yourself an invitation so you'll have a good guess that the mail is on schedule. It's a little peace of mind on the timing of delivery.

Paper invitations should always be used for formal parties and weddings. When tearing open the envelope, guests immediately know that the host is starting early and getting ready. There is considerable time and expense that comes with mailing out real invitations, so do consider that when looking at your budget. If you have a few extra hours and dollars, go for it. It's the best-case scenario.

Invitation Sources

Always look for local sources for stationery. A favorite shop here in Athens, Appointments at Five, is my go-to for Crane & Co. If you don't have a local shop, here are some other sources for personalized stationery that I like:

- Etsy.com: Look online for talented Southern stationery designers
- Papersource.com
- Minted.com

susan and peter

Let's welcome

— THE —

TRIBBLES

back to Athens!

Join us for Cocktails

Thursday 22nd

:30–7:30 p.m.

360 DOGWOOD DRIVE · ATHENS, GEORGIA

Hosted by

MELISSA & BRANDT HALBACH · CATHERINE & LAM HARMON
AMBER & SHILOH HUTTON · REBECCA & KEVIN LANG

RSVP 706.424.0891

Other Channels for Gathering Guests

Y'all come over can be conveyed in many ways and the choices seem to grow all the time. Opting out of paper opens the door to which method works best for you.

Email

Electronic invitations are an easy option and are the most prevalent for less formal events. For email, there are countless sites that gather the email addresses for the guest list, keep up with RSVPs, and even let you know who has opened the email and who has not. Another helpful feature is many sites send a reminder to guests a day or two before the party.

If you're choosing this delivery, make sure to take a look for guests who never opened the email and check in with them. Junk-mail filters can hang these up where guests never see them. There is usually an option for making the guest list and comments public or private. Choose to keep the list private so guests don't feel like they are in a RSVP bubble.

Another way to invite friends over with a keyboard is to compose an email that is memorable and fun to open. This gives guests a little of the same thrill that paper invitations create. Make sure the subject line includes "Invitation" so it stands out in a crowded inbox. Attach a photo or image to an email that has to do with the theme or the guest of honor. For example, for a garden luncheon, I might attach a photo of one my heirloom daffodils. The more personal the invitation, no matter the medium, the better it is.

Messaging on Social Media

Using social media to invite guests depends wholly on the guests, so just be mindful of that when sending invites. I rarely check messages on my social accounts, but your friends may be avid message users. The first step in having people over and making them feel comfortable starts with the invitation. If it works for your friends, go for it.

Texting

There's nothing wrong with a texted invitation if it's for a last-minute party. Spur-of-the-moment gatherings are relaxed and are often the most fun. Many of the electronic invitation companies offer the ability to text as well, which can be a little more exciting to receive than a standard text. If the pop-up party is within two days, texting your friends is fine, but it is not acceptable for parties with longer lead times.

Entertaining Notebook

. . . .

The first large party I ever hosted in our home was not long after we married. We had about 30 guests for dinner and I planned an entrée that had to be cooked at almost the last minute. We also rented a margarita machine but it wouldn't freeze because the crowd stayed in the kitchen, making it extremely warm. I learned a lot that night, including to write down the highs and the lows for next time. The best party givers don't start from scratch each time they plan their next party. It saves so much time when planning the next party because there are notes to refresh your memory.

On your desk, keep a three-ring binder where information about each party can be journaled. Keep the menu, who was invited, who attended, how the bar was set up, and any other details. Maybe you discovered that your grandmother's dessert plates perfectly highlight your new napkins from Target. Add it to your notebook to make sure you remember. Keeping track of what was left over is always helpful to prevent over purchasing next time. Section off the notebook with dividers so each party can be easily found.

Timelines are helpful to include, especially if you now know some time-saving steps for next time. If you have multiple sets of dishes, make a note of which pattern you used and the silverware that went with it. Record the notes the day after the party so no detail is lost to time. Every single entry makes you a better host and gives you a jump start on planning the next soirée.

. . . .

RSVPs

This vital French acronym simply means, "Please reply." It's not an optional choice, it is an obligation of anyone invited. When a host requests an RSVP, it shows an appalling lack of manners to ignore it. In the past, RSVPs were expected in the same form as the invitation. Now, it's very acceptable to use what is most convenient. The invitation should list the preferred method of the RSVP, but if not, just simply communicate with the host in the fashion that you normally would.

Once an invitation is received, an RSVP should be given as soon as possible. Once you RSVP yes or no, you are locked in with that choice. Never should "maybe" be given as a choice (e-invitation services offer this, but don't be tempted). "Maybe" tells the host to prepare for you with food and drink, but you might not show up. I find that worse than not responding.

I do not prefer the option of "Regrets only." It can be confusing for guests and I think commands less urgency than calling for a RSVP.

Shower Etiquette

Showers are some of the most memorable parties, especially for the guest of honor. Many of the same guidelines apply to both baby showers and wedding showers. Here are some guidelines:

⇒ The host should ensure that a notebook is available for a friend of the bride or mother-to-be to write down all gifts and who they are from.
⇒ Anyone who hosts a wedding shower must be invited to the wedding.
⇒ If attending a shower in a home, bring a hostess gift along with your guest of honor gift.
⇒ Invitations for showers should not list where gift registries have been made. The host should be able to let guests know where to find the registries when asked.
⇒ It is never ok to ask guests to self-address envelopes so thank-you note writing is less time-consuming.
⇒ Only family members (and wedding party members) should be invited to multiple showers. Since a gift is expected, most friends should be invited to only one.
⇒ I honestly dread games at showers, but that is the choice of the guest of honor and the host.

Thank-You Notes: Thoughtful Appreciation

No Southern desk should be without stationery and stamps for writing thank-you notes. Whether hosting guests in your home or enjoying hospitality at another house, thank-you notes are essential. And they are greatly appreciated. They should be personal and thoughtful.

No longer than a week should pass before sending a thank-you note. I like to think of three days as prime time for thank-yous, but

No Thank-you for a Thank you

Thank-you notes are not written for receiving hostess gifts. The hostess gift given to you is the thank-you from your guest.

sometimes you will need an extra few days. A late thank-you note is better than no thank-you note. The date should be included on all thank-you notes. The long way of writing out the date is best. For example, November 24, 2021.

Keep pretty stationery in your desk at all times. Thank-you notes can be written only on paper. Other forms of communication are not acceptable. If you need to run out to purchase a notecard each time you should be thanking someone, you're less likely to complete the task. Choose personalized stationery if you can and not the ones that say "Thank you" on the front. You are writing a note so you can say your own "Thank you." If you are especially likely to run short on time, go ahead and have your return address preprinted and even stamp the envelopes in advance.

Stationery: What You Really Pay for

When shopping for stationery, it's easy to get confused about why prices differ so greatly on different choices.

Paper made from cotton is the highest in quality and often the most expensive. No acid is used in the production of paper from cotton, so the paper lasts the longest time before breaking down. If you hope to write letters that will be saved for years to come, choose cotton so your words will last a lifetime.

Paper made from wood is less expensive and isn't as long-lasting since acid is used in the process of production.

The three choices of printing on the stationery also is a large factor in the price. For personalizing stationery, the most expensive choice is engraving. The process uses a die to process a three-dimensional quality. Raised printing uses ink instead of die and is often shinier than die. A standard printed personalization is the least expensive option, but still very much worth it to make your stationery just how you want it.

Extra Info

If there is any other information that can be helpful is always appreciated on the invitation as well. If the location has an unusual or tricky parking situation, let the guests know in advance. Also, inform guests how to enter if they need to pass through a gate to arrive. If you really don't want gifts, include a request for no gifts. Depending on your friends, sometimes a courteous "adults only" is needed so guests know to start looking for sitters. If the party is around the holidays or at a time when many people have family in town, you can let them know that houseguests are also welcome. If this is not specifically mentioned, the only ones invited are those whose names are on the invitation.

Children & Thank-you Notes

Once a child learns to write, a mother cannot thank friends in place of the child's personal thank-you note.

Wording a Toast

Don't stress! There's a difference in making a toast at a wedding reception and raising your glass at a party in your home. The pressure to say something perfect that will be remembered for a lifetime doesn't exist. Toasting in a less formal gathering is festive and simply a way to pass on good cheer.

Toasting Tips

- The best toasts are brief.
- Toast any time of day, not just at evening parties.
- Toast with any beverage, not just alcoholic.
- The host always gives the first toast for the guest of honor.
- To toast the host, the guest of honor or closest friend at the party steps up.
- Even if you're not drinking, raise an empty glass.
- If you are the subject of the toast, do not raise your glass. And there's no need to stand if you're seated, just smile. No Southerner should "drink to yourself."

All-Purpose Southern Toasts

"Life is short, break the rules. Forgive quickly, kiss slowly, love truly, laugh uncontrollably, and never regret anything that makes you smile."

—Mark Twain

"Life is all memory, except for the one present moment that goes by you so quick you hardly catch it going."

—Tennessee Williams

"It doesn't matter if it takes a long time getting there, the point is to have a destination."

—Eudora Welty

Planning for Unexpected Diets and Restrictions

Allergies are a serious issue and shouldn't be overlooked or ignored. Any guest has the responsibility for letting the host know if they have dietary needs or allergies. If a guest has a severe allergy, they should call to let the host know in advance. If it's the first time you're having over a friend, you can always ask them if they have allergies, like seafood or peanuts. Especially if you're planning on serving either.

You will never be able to address all the allergies that exist. The longer I cook, the more allergies I learn about.

For friends who are vegans or vegetarians as well as those with religious diet restrictions, I always try to accommodate them and make sure they can eat enough to leave them feeling satisfied. It is rude for a host to make a guest feel out of place or self-conscious about their dietary needs. It may send you slightly more out of your way than you had planned, but it's necessary.

On the seldom occasion that a picky eater (who is an adult) comes to dine at our house, I don't do anything different at all. Choosing not to eat certain things just because they are new is not my concern to address.

Don't become overwhelmed as more and more food aversions and allergies arise. You just can't cover each one all the time. I've found that if a guest has a restriction, they are well versed on how to handle eating at a party within their boundaries.

Potluck Manners for the Host

Potlucks are meant to be easier on the host than a standard party that often leaves all the cooking to one person. As the host, you should give each guest a good idea of what to bring to the party when you extend the invitation. Offer a generic suggestion, like "a potato side dish" or "an easy dessert." Giving some guidance to each guest makes it easier for them to narrow down what they may want to bring. See page 134 for tips about potluck manners as a guest.

3

Around the House

No matter the home, there are key areas that are vital to
making a party the best it can be. The basics are the same no
matter the square footage within the walls. Things like keeping
a crazy-clean powder room and making sure guests know where
to put their coats and showing off impressive blooms are touches
that are truly appreciated by each person choosing to spend
their time with you. Any area in your house where guests
will be should be inviting and welcoming.

Getting Your House Ready

Don't be ashamed, everyone has done it. It's the manic cleaning burst a few hours before friends are coming over to make your house look like no pets, no children, and really no untidy adults have ever lived there. Closets are jammed, beds are stuffed underneath, even the oven may hold things that don't live in the kitchen. There's only so much you can get done in a short time, so I'm giving you a reprieve, mostly.

I have never once attended a party and thought the furniture was dusty. When you're having a great time, you're not looking at such small things. The host always tends to judge their own home much more than anyone else. The key is to clean several days in advance and just touch up the day of the party. On the party day, I zip around with a cordless mini-vacuum in the rooms where the guests will be and use a duster wand on the most visible furniture.

Spend any available time on the two places that should be really clean: the kitchen and the powder room. No one wants to eat from a kitchen that isn't clean. Wipe down the counters before guests arrive and clean as you cook to keep all the dishes from piling up. Take out the trash. Once the party starts, do not wash dishes in front of guests. They'll think they need to help. The powder room is likely the only place guests will be alone and might have a few minutes of quiet. They will notice if it's not clean. The condition of the powder room is a pretty good reflection of the way you keep house.

Especially for large parties, you will want to deep-clean afterward. The more fun your guests have, the less clean your house is when they leave. I save big chores, like mopping, for the day after.

"The host always tends to judge their own home much more than anyone else."

Catchall for Coats and Purses

You can easily feel like a bellhop when guests are arriving and shedding coats and bags. We have a coat closet near the front door that I make sure is empty before a party starts. I keep about ten heavy wooden coat hangers there. It's close enough I can hang up a guest's coat right away and let them know where they can find it later. Depending on the size of purses, I may put them in the bottom of the coat closet or on our bed. Many times, guests will find their own spot to stash them. Without a coat closet, a rolling rack in a bedroom for coats to be hung is a great option. These can be purchased at home stores and are useful in many situations. (I keep tablecloths hanging from mine when they're not in use for parties.) Although hanging is the best-case scenario, laying coats and jackets neatly on a bed is also a good solution.

Unfortunately, some hosts will have a designated place to leave your shoes before you enter their home. Unless you are attending a party in a yoga studio or on a yacht with all white decks, you should not be asked to remove your shoes. It makes guests uncomfortable worrying about the condition of their socks or quickly counting back to how long has passed since the last pedicure. Of course, stick to your Southern manners and abide by what the host asks of you with a smile on your face, but make a mental note never to ask that of guests at your house.

If rain is in the forecast, plan for an appropriate spot right outside the front door for wet umbrellas. Umbrella stands, baskets, clean tall planters from the garden, and even vintage coolers will work for this. Put one of your umbrellas in the container before party time so everyone knows right away that's the appropriate storage area.

Seldom, guests arrive with bluebird skies and leave during a frog-strangling rain. Just in case, have several extra umbrellas if a guest needs to borrow one when heading out.

The Perfect Powder Room

The one set-in-stone rule for the powder room is that it has to be spotless. This is the only room in the house that follows this rule. Make sure it's well stocked with extra toilet paper, clean towels, and nicely scented hand soap. Either pump hand soap or pretty bars of soap are fine choices. I always keep a fresh hand towel on the towel rack but especially for parties, I like to leave disposable guest towels out on the counter as well. Look for thick, white paper towels that look very similar to linen.

A little bud vase with a small clipping from your yard or a bloom from the grocery store is perfect next to the sink. It takes only a couple of minutes and adds a personal touch. It's the little things like this that guests really appreciate.

Check in on the powder room a few times during the party. You never know when a little tidying is needed.

Make use of chairs all around the house if you need extra seating during a party. Ottomans and stools can do double duty easily for anyone that needs to sit. If elderly guests are coming over, ensure they get a nice comfortable chair where they can partake and enjoy the party as much as everyone else.

Considerate Parking

Depending on where you live, parking can be a difficulty during entertaining. As the host, it should be your hassle and not your guests' or your neighbors'. Give your neighbors a little notice that more cars will be on your street than usual for the event. If there are certain details about parking that guests need to know, make sure to include them on the invitation. Gated communities usually have a guest code, so pass that on in advance so the entrance doesn't get jammed with cars. If a parking deck is involved, let your guests know what level is most convenient to your home. The more details to make getting to the party easier, the better.

Pets

We own the world's cutest dog. She's sweet, loving, friendly, and abnormally soft. I consider her my third child. All that said, she does not attend all parties in her own house. No matter how much you love your pets, every guest in your home may not feel the same. If Cee needs to vacate, I send her to my parents' house, just a few blocks away, or set her up in the basement with lots of chew toys.

An unattractive aspect of partying where pets live is hair. If your house is like mine, the sofa can easily have plenty of hair that you never see until you stand up and it's all over your black pants. Make sure you run the vacuum or a lint roller over the upholstered furniture before guests arrive. They should leave your home filled with good food and drink, not covered in pet hair.

Emergency Party Cleaning

There will be a spill eventually at a party so be prepared to address it discreetly but quickly.

Wine stains are the most dreaded, by both hosts and guests. One way to head off party stain disasters is to have upholstered furniture and carpet treated with stain preventative treatment at the time of purchase.

For red wine on table linens, artificial sweetener works wonders. If the wine has soaked through the tablecloth and is in contact with the table, place a kitchen towel under the cloth to prevent the wine from damaging the finish of the table. Pile artificial sweetener on the stain and allow it to sit for 12 hours. The sweetener will absorb much of the stain. Brush off the sweetener and use distilled white vinegar to further scrub the stain (if the cloth is a cotton or cotton blend). Wash as usual.

White wine on table linens can be removed with club soda before washing as usual. While these stains are less noticeable when they happen, they can cause yellowing long-term if left untreated.

Offer to help guests that have spilled on their clothing so they don't feel awkward moving about the party with a stain. Ask the guest if they would like a white towel and club soda to treat their stain. Also offer a private space in your home so they can tackle the spill without an audience.

Red wine spilled on carpet is the worst-case scenario for a party spill. Jump right on it to prevent long-term damage. Pour water or white wine over the red stain to prevent it from setting. Pile a generous layer of table salt on the stain and cover with a wet, but not soaking, white towel. At this point, the party goes on. After the last guest has gone home, use white towels to blot (never rub) the stain until you see no more remnants of the stain on the towels. If the stain remains to be stubborn, keep the stain wet (do not allow the carpet to dry) until a professional service can arrive. A stain that hasn't dried is much easier to remove than one that has.

As with all surfaces and fabrics, make sure you abide by what the manufacturer recommends for cleaning.

Small Space Entertaining

Entertaining well has nothing to do with square footage. Some of the best parties are thrown in small apartments in large cities (think of Holly Golightly's epic festivities) and in cozy, petite homes everywhere. These gatherings tend to be more intimate, charming, and encourage guests to interact more with each other. Even though there's less space for capacity, a bit of creativity and planning makes every inch work.

Moving furniture around and repurposing what you have is a good place to start. Just about anything can be turned into a bar. A coffee table with cushions around it makes an unexpected dining table. A few folding chairs go a long way. They are inexpensive to rent and free to borrow. Handled trays make any lap an instant table. When you see good trays on sale, pick some up for the next party. A folding TV tray is one of the best small space entertaining tools you can have. It can become virtually anything from a serving piece, a bar, or an intimate table for two.

Creating a small space and focusing on one room or area, even within a large home, can turn any get-together into an intimate gathering. With smaller guest lists or close friends, encourage guests to congregate in the kitchen or on a porch or an airy sunroom. With food and wine nearby, friends are unlikely to wander off.

Outdoor Entertaining

Even the most talented event designers can't replace the elegance and ambiance of an outdoor party. A setting with birds chirping, trees slightly swaying in the wind, and natural light is priceless.

The first consideration on whether to plan your gathering indoors or outdoors is, of course, based on the weather. Here, in Georgia, it may be too hot to be outside or so humid that your hair soon takes on a new life. Unless there's a porch with a really wide roof, the rain will keep your gathering inside for sure. If you're considering hosting outside, go ahead and let guests know that, weather permitting, you'll be dining outdoors. They will appreciate the heads up for choosing clothing. Arrange the bar and food, if possible, outside to prevent guests from having to come inside and out each time they need a refill.

Cleaning is less of a chore for outdoor parties. The powder room is still a must for keeping clean, but with guests outside, you can be more relaxed on the details of everywhere else. Keep a lightweight battery-powered blower that you can quickly zip around before the party to remove any leaves or debris. If it's pollen season, try a handheld vacuum on the porch and patio. Pollen can be a nemesis for outdoor spring parties, but I've found a vacuum is much more effective than a broom.

"A setting with birds chirping, trees slightly swaying in the wind, and natural light is priceless."

Leaf 'N Petal

A Southern home should never be without a fresh flower. Blooms are a weakness of mine, for no other reason than they make me happy. My grandmother was a talented florist, but her flower shop (named Leaf 'N Petal) closed before I was old enough to appreciate it. I so wish that wasn't the case. I often pick up flowers at the grocery store, divide up the bunch and mix them with clippings from my yard to enjoy. Never, ever would I have a party without flowers.

Having fun vessels is part of the adventure. Vases and containers of all kinds can be collected throughout the years. I try to pick up bud vases when I travel so I have unique arrangements that hold good memories.

Purchasing flowers isn't always necessary. Depending on the time of year, clip from your yard (or from your friends' yards) for blooms and greenery. When you're shopping for plants at the nursery, think about if some of those plants will be good for snipping and putting in arrangements. Herbs make great additions in little vases and they are always growing in our yard. Ewe, ferns, and cryptomeria are just a few of the versatile choices that are easy to grow and add texture in flower arrangements.

Daffodils, camellias, magnolia, hydrangeas, and azaleas tend to bloom and show off all over the South. Many Southern women are known to ride around with clippers in their car just in case they see a blooming plant in desperate need of "pruning" (always with permission, of course).

When the flowers you have in mind aren't right outside your door, look for those that are more economical and last a long time. Daisies, sunflower, chrysanthemum, gerbera daisies, and alstroemeria are normally low in cost and have a really long life in a vase. Several stems of silver dollar eucalyptus in a vase is surprisingly elegant and very inexpensive. Look for bouquets labeled "filler" at the grocery store. They are normally pretty and cost very little.

Don't limit your choices to just flowers. Artichokes, pears, apples, cabbages, and lemons are just a few of the edibles that make stunning centerpieces.

Especially for entertaining, consider the fragrance of flowers. For parties, flowers should be seen, not smelled, near the food. I steer clear of lilies for this reason.

> "Don't limit your choices to just flowers. Artichokes, pears, apples, cabbages, and lemons are just a few of the edibles that make stunning centerpieces."

Tools

····

Sharp Hand Clippers:
The mainstay of any flower
arrangement. Get an extra
pair for your car.

Snips: Tiny stems take tiny
blades and work easily on
springs to open and close.

Flower Scissors: Tender
stems benefit from ultra-sharp
ceramic-bladed scissors.

Flower Food: When stirred in
the water, blooms will last longer
and the water will stay cleaner.

Stemming Machine: I inherited
my grandmother's from Leaf 'N
Petal, but splurge on your own
for the easiest wreath making
ever (right).

Never leave behind a mint julep cup at an estate sale. The versatility of this infamous cup is endless. Not only are they the vessel for one of the South's most famous cocktails, they are the perfectly sized classy little vase for flowers. The small cups normally fit well in the powder room, the bar, and any little side table that needs a pop of color. The silver is weighty enough that arrangements won't become top-heavy and turn over.

Longer Life for Flowers

» Those little packets of powdered floral food really do work. Flowers will stay fresher for longer.
» Remove leaves that will be below the waterline.
» Change the water every 2 to 3 days and make a fresh cut on the bottom of the stems.
» Keep arrangements away from direct sunlight and direct airflow.
» Use warm water when filling vases.
» Make a cross cut on woody stems to help water absorption.
» Add one aspirin to dissolve in the water for roses.

Perking up a Sad Flower

You may not be able to save every drooping bloom, but you can try. Here are some tips to help:

» Recut the stems and replace in fresh water to see if they perk up.
» Place the entire flower in a container of water slightly warmer than room temperature for 30 minutes.
» Wipe the stems of wild flowers dry and then let them sit in white vinegar for 5 to 10 minutes.

The $20 Statement Bouquet

Create a lush, artistic look by pairing greenery
(snipped straight from the yard) with a few
dramatic blooms. Secure loose stems with
florist wire, and wrap with twine.

MATERIALS: mixed bouquet + greenery + florist wire + twine

THE VASE: any tall glass cylinder

Candle Sense

For some hosts, candles are as much as a part of entertaining as food and drink. A flame during a party adds a beautiful glow to anywhere its light reaches. And, as an added bonus, everyone looks better in candlelight. Before electricity was common and candles were a necessity, there were a few etiquette rules that came along with open flames. Once a new candle was placed in a candelabra or a candle stick, the wick was burned immediately, even if only for a few seconds. Having candles displayed in the home with a new wick was a sure sign you lived with the luxury of electricity. Many Southerners preferred to keep their electricity usage to themselves, at least until it was more common.

Only unscented candles should be used around food or during a party. Any scent can distract from the meal and even cause some guests with sensitive allergies a problem. Save the scented candles for relaxing at home when there's not a crowd coming over.

Candles make lovely hostess gifts, especially the more beautifully packaged versions. When choosing a candle for a gift, opt for light, delicate scents. The more approachable the scent means the more likely the host will like the way it smells. An outdoor party isn't a party without a candle. I still like to stick to the unscented versions, even in open air.

Candle height is something to consider when using them on the dining table. The flame should not be directly at eye level. When guests are seated, the light shouldn't be shining directly into their eyes. The last item on the to-do list before the first doorbell ring is to light the candles. When using candles on the table, discreetly light the candles before everyone sits down to eat.

Don't stress if any candle wax is dripped on table linens during dinner. After guests have gone, place the linen in the freezer to make removal of the wax easier. Once it's cold, the wax can be cracked and removed. Mineral spirits can remove any oily residue left on the cloth. Pour rubbing alcohol over to "rinse" and allow to dry. Wash as usual.

"Only unscented candles should be used around food or during a party."

Music is a Must!

Sign up for a music streaming service to make party tunes a breeze or put together a playlist. Here are some ideas for classic, no-fail playlists.

Hits from the 60's

"Your Love Keeps Lifting Me Higher and Higher" by Jackie Wilson

"Shout" by the Isley Brothers

"My Girl" by the Temptations

"You've Lost That Lovin' Feelin'" by the Righteous Brothers

"Brown Eyed Girl" by Van Morrison

"Lord, You Are My Adorable One" by Bishop Joe Simon

"Joy to the World" by Three Dog Night

"Good Lovin'" by the Young Rascals

"(You Make Me Feel like) A Natural Woman" by Aretha Franklin

"Gimme Some Lovin'" by the Spencer Davis Group

"You Can't Always Get What You Want" by the Rolling Stones

"It's the Same Old Song" by the Four Tops

"Apple, Peaches, Pumpkin Pie" by Jay & the Techniques

"Carolina Girls" by General Johnson & the Chairmen of the Board

"You Can't Hurry Love" by the Supremes

Jazz

"Take Five" by the Dave Brubeck Quartet

"Giant Steps" by John Coltrane

"Gospel Groove" by Shuggie Otis

"West End Blues" by Louis Armstrong & His Hot Five

"In a Sentimental Mood" by Duke Ellington and John Coltrane

"Someday My Prince Will Come" by Miles Davis

"Cantaloupe Island" by Herbie Hancock

"All My Loving" by Count Basie

"Royal Garden Blues" by Charlie Christian

"Pennies from Heaven" by the Dave Brubeck Quartet

"Secret Love" by Joe Pass

"How High the Moon" by the Modern Jazz Quartet

"Newport Blues" by Dizzy Gillespie

"Light Blue" by Thelonious Monk Quartet

"Honeysuckle Rose" by Stephane Grappelli

Southern Rock

"Bad Moon Rising" by Creedence Clearwater Revival

"Ramblin' Man" by the Allman Brothers Band

"Can't You See" by the Marshall Tucker Band

"Sweet Home Alabama" by Lynyrd Skynyrd

"Keep Your Hands to Yourself" by the Georgia Satellites

"Midnight Rider" by Gregg Allman

"Coming Home" by Johnny Van Zant Band

"Guitar Town" by Steve Earle

"Fooled Around and Fell in Love" by Elvin Bishop

"Life's Been Good" by Joe Walsh

"Flirtin' with Disaster" by Molly Hatchet

"Keep on Smilin'" by Wet Willie

"Jackie Blue" by the Ozark Mountain Daredevils

"Good One Comin' On" by Blackberry Smoke

"The Devil Went Down to Georgia" by the Charlie Daniels Band

4

At the Door

If I could count the times that my mom told my sister and me growing up, "You only have one chance to make a first impression," I'd be a math genius. Those few moments before a guest rings the doorbell or knocks to announce their arrival are precious. Making the door lovely on the outside is as important as the warm welcome that's waiting on inside. Who would have ever thought that wreaths, potted plants, and a proper introduction would go together so well?

Designating a Door

Some homes have more than one door on the front of the house. Townhomes and apartments sometimes have more than one choice of entrances. If that's the case, make it clear to guests which door is appropriate to avoid any confusion. There are several ways to designate a door. Proper lighting and decor can both be a good indication your friends are in the right place.

Years ago, we lived in a house with a back door that was more accessible than our front door (thanks to living on a steep hill). My husband and I hosted a Christmas party and almost everyone came in the back door, just like they would any other time. My lights were on at the front door and the entrance leading up to it, but my mistake was leaving the light on at the back door. Had the lights been turned off in the back of the house, the lights at the front would be the indication that the front door was preferred.

Using decor like a wreath on the door or planters nearby are also a clue on the right entrance. In the fall, arrange pretty pumpkins and gourds near the entrance. Another option is paper bag luminaries with sand and battery-operated tea lights. They are a classic added touch leading up to the door.

The First Impression

The first step inside a home represents the first impression each guest will have of any event. The threshold should be clean and the door and surrounding windows free of spiderwebs and dust. Check the doorbell and make sure it works. The tiny lightbulb inside the doorbell button should be shining. Easily seeing where to ring the bell makes a big difference for first-time guests.

Make the front door as approachable and attractive as possible. Add some pretty, large ferns on either side of the door. I buy Macho ferns at the grocery store and keep them in the original pots. I can easily swap them out of containers before parties. The pathway up to the door should be well-lit and easy to walk.

"Both proper lighting and decor show your friends that they are in the right place."

The Right Wreath

When choosing a wreath to adorn the door, consider the size to make sure the wreath is in proportion. A wreath that is too large can be overpowering on a door and get caught in the frame as the door closes. An especially full wreath can also create a little havoc in the hair of those that cross over the threshold.

The choice of where to place the bow is up to you. (If you want a bow at all.) The measurement of a wreath is the diameter from the outside edge to the opposite outside edge. For standard 36-inch doors, a 24-inch wreath is the most common choice. When hanging a wreath, the top of the wreath should be 13 to 14 inches below the top of the door. A 36-inch wreath is usually best for larger, oversized doors.

Manning the Door

At least one of the hosts should be near the front door as guests arrive. Each person that walks into your home should be greeted and know that they are welcome immediately. It's an unsettling feeling to arrive at a party and finally cross paths with the host 30 minutes later. Avoid having the appearance of a receiving line as guests come in. Reserve those for weddings and funerals. Casually remain close to the entrance until everyone has arrived.

If you're on the other side of the door and arriving as a guest, try to be conscious of speaking to the host but not taking up too much time. As more guests arrive, they also need to be welcomed as well. When it's time to go home, make sure to thank the host for having you and say a thoughtful goodbye as you exit.

The Best Flow

People talk about the flow of parties a lot, but they often don't know what makes a flow work or why it fails miserably. Several factors, not just the layout of your house, determine the success of party flow.

The flow is the most important at the beginning of a party and at the moment the food is served, especially if it's a buffet. It also can change depending on who the guests are and even what the weather is outside. My home has a wide front porch. If the weather is pleasant, guests tend to mingle on the porch, so I like to put a bar out there so everyone is happy. If it's cold, company comes right on inside and things are different and the flow must adjust.

The key to a good flow is to avoid a bottleneck or congestion anywhere in the house. Walk into your home as a guest would and imagine how it would be to arrive for the first time. Think about the easiest path to move as you walk around. I've even had friends over to give their opinion. It's sometimes hard to look at the functionality of your home with a fresh eye. You can also direct the flow of traffic with bar placement. Guests move to a drink every time. In a home setting, no one expects a line at the bar of more than two or three people. You may find that you want a tray with a signature cocktail near the entrance and a larger bar selection further into the house or on the back patio.

The food shouldn't be too close to the bar so there is room between the two to move about. Other spots that tend to have traffic flow issues can be where the coats are stored, any narrow entrances into rooms, and right inside the front door.

Etiquette of Introductions

The responsibility of introducing guests to each other usually comes along with the job of hosting the party. Keeping a few things in mind helps to make the smoothest introductions for all involved. Here are a few tips:

» When introducing a couple, use both of their first names (Kevin and Rebecca Lang), not just "The Langs."

» Offer an introduction phrase like "I'd like you to meet…" and not "Have you met?" or "Do you know?" to begin the introduction. If they actually have met but one doesn't remember, it can be awkward.

» Hopefully the two people you are introducing to each other will have something in common that you can mention to help start the conversation between them.

» The more often you can repeat the names of those you are introducing, the more likely it is the names will be remembered.

» If being introduced and you are not 100% sure you haven't met before, say "It's nice to see you" instead of "It's nice to meet you."

» If someone has gotten your name wrong, politely correct them and change the subject quickly.

Gifts for Guests

Sending guests on their way with a little take-home present is not necessary, but if given, it should be memorable. When I attend a party, I see the food, drinks, and the hospitality as the gift from the host, so I never expect to leave with anything extra. If you do choose to go the extra mile and send home a goodie, think of items that may tie in with the theme or type of party. For brunch, a little jar of fig preserves would be nice. For a party that's going to go strong until late at night, small bags of ground coffee might make the morning easier. The faux pas with parting gifts happens when you give items that would be free or deeply discounted for you. For example, if you own a candle company, avoid giving your candles to your guests as gifts.

Handling a Rude or Tipsy Guest

Sometimes unpleasant things happen at a party. If a guest is offensive or overserved to the point of ridiculousness, go to his or her spouse, date, or friend (if they are going to be of any help) to tactfully and quietly aid in the exit. If no "better half" is present, ask a good friend of yours to assist. All should be done as inconspicuously and graciously as possible.

Never allow a guest to drive home who shouldn't. When someone is overserved at your house, you have to take responsibility. Insist on a comfortable stay in your guest room for the night or call a car to safely make the delivery home.

When and How to End a Party

Most parties have a natural and organic end to them. Guests find themselves full, happy, and become conscious of the party coming to a close. But, once in a while, you might have a lingerer, even one you really like. But, no matter how long the last guest stays, hold off cleaning until the door closes for the very last time. It's the same concept you've heard growing up. Just because someone else doesn't have the best manners doesn't give you the excuse to let yours slip. To help, here are some exit strategies:

≫ Offering coffee is the easiest signal that the end is near. The coffee cup is empty, and it's time to go home.

≫ If you have your lights on a dimmer (which I'm a huge fan of) and you have most of them at half power for mood, gradually turn them up. As the room gets brighter, guests will meander toward the door.

≫ Do not continue to refill alcoholic drinks if you're really hinting at an exit. The closing of a bar is a good clue.

≫ Ask if anyone would like to take a few leftovers home with them. But be conscious not to overload them with servings for the next day.

≫ Begin speaking in past tense, "Wasn't tonight such a fun time?"

5

On the Table

Being welcomed at the table is nothing short of receiving a
special gift. The all-important table can easily become a vital
element of parties and festivities in countless and amazing ways.
It doesn't matter if the table is a priceless antique or a temporary
place for a meal, it's the epicenter of hospitality. When you
are sitting at our table, you are family. It's the place for
guests to gather, laugh, eat and plan to do it all over
again. Pulling up a chair is just the beginning.

Setting a Table with Personality

The way you dress reflects your personality just like the way you choose to decorate your home echoes who you are. Think of your table in the exact same way. Use family heirlooms and new pieces you purchased at the same time. One of the best ways to start a conversation during a meal is by telling the story of what's on the table. Silverware can be an eclectic mix as well, but it's best to keep the same pattern for each person.

Starting with the Shape

The shape of the table is the first factor in choosing how to set the table. Rectangle, oval, and round tables should be treated differently to make the most of their dimensions.

Round

For a round table, everyone will be focused on the center of the table. A large, low centerpiece will work perfectly to draw eyes in but not hamper conversation. One benefit of a round table is that it's often easier for left-handed guests to eat comfortably.

Oval

Oval tables are the hardest to find linens for that fit properly. Take advance of this and make the place settings standout with bright napkins and interesting plates. An oval container for a centerpiece, like a vintage bread bowl, works wonderfully. Or try several bud vases to make an impact.

Rectangle

A long rectangular table is an ideal shape to show off a pretty table runner and make a low, lengthy centerpiece. Each long side of the table should be a mirror image of the other.

How to Use a Table Pad Under a Tablecloth
. . . .

A table pad helps the look of how a tablecloth drapes from the edges of the table. It also can help absorb sound and protects the table from scratches, heat, and spills. Many vintage table pads are foldable (like an accordion) for storage with one side of felt and one side of vinyl. Newer ones can be made of polyester and latex and come in a roll to be cut to fit. If ever you buy an antique table and it comes with the original table pads, you have lucked out!

Elements of a Casual Table

Comfort and approachability are at the forefront of casual tables.
They can be more relaxed by using less sheen like choosing
stainless steel instead of silver. Pewter and tin give muted metal
feel that is welcoming and relaxed. Chargers of any material are
a nice way to add layer and warmth to each place setting. Cotton
napkins and simple glasses round out the ultimate laid-back table.

Elements of a More Formal Table

A stunning formal table is elegant and should entice guests to sit and partake. Crystal and silver at each place setting reflect candlelight and add glow to each inch of the table. Place cards are nice for formal tables to add extra decor to each seat and for helping guests to easily find their place. Linen napkins and place mats are dressy and classic for almost any occasion, but you can also use a tablecloth. Adding more silverware and bread and butter plates makes meals more of a memorable experience for each and every guest. Tables are more than a piece of furniture. They are one of the few places where all stresses and upsets are set aside for the simple pleasure of a meal with others. Our dining room table was the same table that my grandmother grew up around. It is, by far, my most cherished possession. One reason I love to entertain is to bring friends together at this very table.

Seating for Serendipity

Place Cards

If you're having more than eight guests, use place cards to help them find their seat easily. Place cards make guests feel especially welcomed and can be more formal or casual depending on the materials used—you'll find lots of inspiration on the next pages. There's no need to buy holders; just about anything can be turned into a place card. Just keep in mind who you place next to each other for the best conversation.

Place cards should be an element to the table, not an afterthought. They can be made to be so beautiful that guests want to take them home as a keepsake. Consider that a compliment to the looks of the table. When adornments (like little potted plants here) are used as an element of the place card, guests are encouraged to take them home as a gift from the host.

Escort Cards

Mostly used at weddings and large events, escort cards are often found outside of an event or party and they list the name of each guest and the table number where they will be seated. This upfront organizing creates a much faster and less chaotic process to having all guests settled in their seats. Everyone then has a clear idea of where they are going once they enter the room.

"There's no need to buy holders:
just about anything can be
turned into a place card."

Table Linen Talk

Napkin Basics

Napkins are as essential as food and drink when entertaining. When buying cloth napkins, look for permanent-press fabric to save on ironing. You can never go wrong adding a monogram to a simple cloth or choosing colorful patterns that can liven up a table instantly.

It's distracting to the meal when the napkins have a strong scent of detergent. Keep some unscented laundry soap, if it's not your normal brand, to use for table linens. No lipstick should be on napkins. If possible, guests should discreetly blot their lipstick with a tissue before sitting down to eat.

For the Perfect Size

· · · · · · · · · · · · · · · · ·

Dinner: 22 inches square
Luncheon: 14 inches square
Cocktail: 4 inches square

· · · · · · · · · · · · · · · · ·

Monogram Primer

Monograms are a staple of the Southern home. They're an opportunity to add color and interest and show off your style. Here are a few tips to consider when deciding how to monogram your linens:

1. For optimum visibility, place a monogram in the left corner of a napkin. When folded in a triangle, it will appear at the napkin's point, or, when folded as a rectangle, on the lower outside corner.

2. Ivory-with-gold is the classic "little black dress" of the tabletop. It works whether china is white, bone, or something unexpected.

3. Express your personality on cocktail napkins by pairing bold colors and interesting motifs.

4. A monogram can be so much more than simply initials. Add borders— like this old-world ring stitch—or other unique decorative touch.

5. Hand towels aren't just for the powder room; use them as oversize napkins. They look so pretty draped over chair backs.

6. When monogramming your place mats, keep the insignia in a conspicuous place, such as the top, to keep it from getting covered by plates and glassware once the table is set.

7. Keep it simple. A stacked sans serif font makes a handsome, unfussy choice for modern cocktail napkins.

8. For a graphic, less traditional look, choose a cipher design that interlocks the leading letters of a couple's first names.

9. Using the last initial only gives linens a more contemporary vibe.

10. Don't be afraid to go bold in the color of the linen or the monogram—or both. It adds interest and a bit of fun to your table.

11. Don't worry about matching every monogram in the house. Each different one shows a bit of your personality.

Tablecloth Tactics

A really good tablecloth is just about priceless. With one swoosh, the table is transformed. Keeping tablecloths clean, storing them properly, and choosing the right size makes all the difference in owning lifetime heirlooms and temporary decorations.

Sizing up Your Table

Tablecloths are sold in mostly standard sizes, but tables are not. To make the best choice on size, do a little math to find out what works best for you. (If determining size is too much of a hassle, choose place mats or a table runner instead. They can stand alone on a table.)

The part of the cloth that hangs off the table is called the drop. Eight to 16 inches should fall from the edge of the table. A shorter drop is more casual and is easier on those sitting around the table (so the cloth doesn't pool in their lap). The more formal a party is, the longer the drop becomes. Sharpen your pencil to measure your table and get the perfect-sized cloth.

For the Perfect Size

Rectangular or Square Table:
Measure the width and length of the table.
• Width of table + (cloth drop x 2)
• Length of table + (cloth drop x 2)

Round Table:
Measure the diameter of the table.
• Diameter of table + (cloth drop x 2)

Napkin Folds

The Bow Tie Fold

1. Lay the napkin flat. Fold the opposite sides inward to meet in the center.

2. Fold at the center to make a narrower rectangle.

3. Fold the short ends back to meet in the center.

4. Cinch in the middle with a ribbon or piece of fabric. Secure in the back with ¾-inch of double-side fabric tape.

The Pocket Fold

1. For the best results, it's best to first iron your napkins thoroughly to ensure a more rigid finish. Fold the napkin in half and then into quarters.

2. Fold the top-most layer of the napkin in half diagonally.

3. Turn the napkin over. Fold the right side back about one-third of the way.

4. Fold the left side over one-third of the way over the other side and tuck the end into the pocket.

The Knotted Napkin

1. Loosely tie a knot in the center of a napkin.

2. Set it off-center on the plate.

3. Cut paper tags for place cards, and write a guest's name on each one.

4. Tuck the place card on the plate underneath the knotted napkin.

Folding Napkins

Classic napkin folds arranged on the plate are my favorite. I make napkin rings out of twine or fresh herbs or vines, and don't own traditional napkin rings. There are endless ways to personalize the napkin and make it yours.

Cleaning Napkins and Tablecloths

Never apply heat (a clothes dryer or an iron) to stained linens. The warmth will set the stain permanently. Make sure you've treated all stains before washing. Unscented detergent is best to use for all tables linens.

Stain Pains
. . . .

Lipstick can be removed from napkins with rubbing alcohol. Make a small stack of three paper towels. Lay the napkin on top of the paper towel, with the lipstick stain touching the paper towel (stain-side down). Dab the underside of the stain with rubbing alcohol and the lipstick will transfer to the paper towel. This may take several dabs to remove completely.

Greasy stains are best removed with dishwashing soap or dishwasher detergent mixed with water. I especially like a paste made from my powdered dishwasher detergent. Use a soft toothbrush to work the paste into the stain.

Removing **wine** is easiest done over a sink. As soon as possible after the spill, place a colander under the section of the cloth that is stained and pull the cloth taut across the top of the colander (a rubber band or chip clips work well for this). Apply a very thick layer of table salt on the stain and allow to stand 10 minutes. While the salt stands, bring 4 cups of water to a boil. Pour boiling water directly onto the salt. If you can, hold the pot or kettle several inches above the cloth to create more water pressure to wash away the stain.

White Linens That Have Yellowed Combine oxygen-based bleaching detergent and very warm water. Submerge linens in the solution overnight to brighten.

. . . .

Storing Linens

Store linens only after they are completely clean, dry, ironed, and ready for use again. I like to hang tablecloths on an empty clothes rack in my basement. My napkins are stored in a large drawer in my kitchen, so they are easily accessible.

Linen Rental

There's a lot to be said for renting table linens and not having the responsibility of cleaning and storing them. It can be much less expensive than buying linens that you may not use often. Most online rental outlets give you the choice to choose the fabric, color, design, and, of course, the size of table linens. Make sure you get a quote on the exact linens you want, as more elaborate fabrics will cost more. The linens are often shipped to you ready to use and can be shipped back for the company to clean. Renting napkins removes all the pressure of washing and pressing for next time. When ordering napkins, add a few extra on the final number in case of spills throughout the event.

Getting Food on the Table

How you serve at the table is best decided by the formality of the event and how many people you have on hand to help you. Plating food in the kitchen and bringing it out to the table is very time-consuming but is nothing short of stunning. The more helpers you have, the easier this style is to manage. It's best for formal events and fancier parties.

Conversation Woes

If conversation lulls or steers in a bumpy direction, be prepared to steer things down a different path. Southern manners should be at their best while around the table. Always be interested in the ideas of your company and what they have to say. Your grandmother probably said this and it's still true: The table is no place to talk about politics or religion. This becomes even more important the less you know about your guests. Gossip is also poor form while dining. It's often said in the South that you never know who is related to whom. Keep this in mind (especially if you just moved here).

Table Manners Refresher

Most Southern children have had more lessons in table manners than they care to remember. But, revisiting a few main points can be helpful for adults.

- There should be nothing on the table that isn't required for eating. That includes phones.

- Once the napkin has been placed in your lap, it should never return to the tabletop. If you must get up from the table, leave the napkin in your seat. Getting up from your chair and returning is best done from the right side. Especially with a lot of chairs around the table, it keeps things a little more orderly.

- The salt and pepper shakers should always be passed together.

Kid's Table

Plan for Children

If children are on the guest list, plan for them to have fun too. Seating children at a separate table can make dining a little more relaxed for the adults and be extra fun for the kids. Don't put their table too far away. It's important for children to learn how to behave at the table, so let them sit close enough to the grown-ups to observe.

Set the table similarly, but not as elaborately, as you would set the adult table. Plastic or melamine are great options for the kids' tables. If the children are old enough, let them choose what's on the table and allow them to set it. The more practice, the better!

Big family holidays, like Christmas, Thanksgiving, and Easter, bring out the most need for children's tables. If a child is feeling too old to sit at the kids' table, it's probably time to join the grown-ups. Never, ever seat an adult at the kids' table. You can always find another chair from somewhere to make room for another adult at the dining table.

Keeping Them Busy

Sitting and chatting isn't going to keep the party going for the little people. The table needs activities to hold attention. The easiest way to do this is by laying a large piece of craft paper on the table (as you would a tablecloth) and letting them go to town with crayons. Bowls of stickers are usually a hit as well as pretty containers of Lego pieces (if the children are over 3). If you're eating outside and the sun is setting, add glow sticks to the table for neon fun. When kids are entertained, parents are better at being guests.

For Christmas, look for fun activities, like filling clear, plastic ornaments with fun trinkets for the tree. Craft paper works wonders at Thanksgiving too for children to write down all they are thankful for. Any holiday craft that's easy for little hands and not too messy can work for just about any celebration.

The Art of the Open House

The Southern open house party is one unlike any others. These types of parties can go by many names, like open house, come and go, or drop-in. A range of time, usually 2 or 3 hours, is given on the invitation so guests know what the window is for stopping by. Usually very light fare is offered like a punch and a few small bites of both savory and sweet.

Open houses are usually hosted in honor of someone, such as a newly married couple that have just started their life together. An after-graduation gathering for friends to congratulate the new graduate or a welcome to town for a new neighbor are other fine examples. Things to remember when hosting an open house:

» The crowd will ebb and flow. Some blocks of time may be crowded and some may be empty.

» Have food and drink fresh and refilled throughout the entire time frame. For guests arriving in the last 30 minutes, the offerings should be as enticing as they were in the first few minutes.

» You can invite more guests than for a standard party since they will be present at different times.

Parties and the Junior League and Garden Clubs

Junior Leagues and garden clubs across the country have played important roles of entertaining for generations. Meetings hosted in homes were the catalyst to thrust young women into the roll of hostess, ready or not. In the past, meetings of these groups would be fairly elaborate with china and silver on full display. Now, meetings may be held in offices and public facilities, but when the location is in a home, the tradition of hospitality continues.

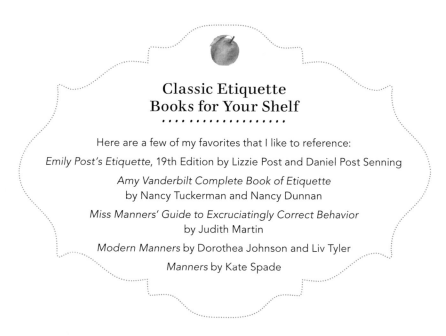

Classic Etiquette Books for Your Shelf

Here are a few of my favorites that I like to reference:

Emily Post's Etiquette, 19th Edition by Lizzie Post and Daniel Post Senning

Amy Vanderbilt Complete Book of Etiquette
by Nancy Tuckerman and Nancy Dunnan

Miss Manners' Guide to Excruciatingly Correct Behavior
by Judith Martin

Modern Manners by Dorothea Johnson and Liv Tyler

Manners by Kate Spade

Eating Outdoors in the South

We all learned new ways to appreciate eating outside during the past year. Dining outdoors quickly went from a special occasion to a necessary delight. One of the very few benefits of having to avoid indoor social gatherings has been learning to embrace the art of eating outside. Now that we all know how fun it can be, we can perfect how we make it truly memorable.

I adore melamine plates and use them almost all spring and summer in my kitchen even when I'm not having guests. Look for substantial plates that are about ¼ inch thick. Durable melamine is BPA-free, shatterproof, dishwasher safe on the top rack, and even scratch-resistant.

Choosing where guests will eat is important. Tables or any seating should be in the shade if at all possible. Take note of which areas of your yard or porch are shaded at what time of day. Plan a party only for a time that a large enough outdoor portion is shaded to accommodate guests. If the weather is chilly outside, consider renting heaters or making use of the fire pit you rarely use.

Even with a sunny weather report, the South is known for humidity and pop-up showers. Always have a rain plan, even if it's just in the back of your mind. Keep any eye on the weather radar starting about an hour before a party to make sure the sky stays clear. Place family-friendly insect repellant out for guests to use. Mosquitos can ruin an outdoor party faster than a thunderstorm.

"Even with a sunny weather report, the South is known for humidity and pop-up showers. Always have a rain plan."

Inspiration from Nature

Use the natural colors of greens and browns or brightly colored blooms to inspire the look and feel of your table. Bringing together slabs of wood and a natural floral arrangement works perfectly paired with a wool throw blanket turned into a tablecloth. Remember the extras that can make outdoor dining totally comfortable, like blankets or insect repellant. Make sure guests are aware that they will be eating outside so they can dress accordingly.

6

On the Buffet

One of my favorite things to say to my guests is, "Y'all go fix
your plates." It's my equivalent of a buffet dinner bell. I love the
look of the stacks of plates and piles of silverware framing out
the array of food for everyone to enjoy. Buffets are beautiful and
comfortable and completely approachable. Even for a simple
weeknight supper, food looks prettier on a platter
with a serving spoon.

The Benefits of a Buffet

A plated dinner is elegant for a small gathering but a buffet is gracious for a crowd. There is no easier way to serve a group than with a buffet. I often serve buffets on my kitchen island so the table is free for seating. It feels more casual to place food out for friends in this way and is more approachable for them since they can choose exactly what they want on their plates. This style works for just about any kind of menu as guests can come and go with plates anytime. Because the buffet is ready at one time, hosts can relax and enjoy the meal like everyone else.

Buffets are functional for the hosts, comfortable for the guests, and can be gorgeous in appearance. Using serving pieces that all coordinate (matching is not required) and laying out the flow to be easy for guests is a must. Every dish should have its own serving utensil. Plates, glasses, napkins, and silverware can be too much to handle while trying to fill and balance a plate, so arrange them in a fashion that is approachable for guests. I like plates at the front with everything else at the end.

No matter how small the area, a buffet can be adjusted to fit. Using small serving dishes and staggering how food is arranged can make the most of every inch. A buffet that is too large can make food look lost, so aim for large platters and bowls to fill the space. Holiday buffets like Thanksgiving, Easter, and Christmas, where there is likely to be a main entrée that needs carving, can really be the time to make a beautiful presentation. Buffets simply are a comfortable choice for nearly every occasion.

rosemary
vinaigrette

shaved
brussel
salad

roasted
potatoes

grilled
asparagus

Gauging How Much Your Guests Will Eat

No host ever wants to run out of food, but you also probably don't want to nibble on party leftovers for the next several days either. Considering a few details can help in deciding how much your guests will eat. Just like making a guesstimate on how much they will drink, there's no exact magic number that applies to everyone, but there are good guidelines.

What is on the social calendar before or after can make a difference. I hosted a brunch the morning after a very late night for many of our friends, and they ate much less than normal (due to not feeling their best). Not in all cases, of course, but in general, men eat larger portions than women. A lunch for ladies requires much smaller portions than a tailgate party loaded with men watching football. Supper is often the meal with the largest portions.

The more the menu includes, the less of each item your guests will eat. Here are some guidelines to get you started:

For the Perfect Size
. . . .

Appetizers (before a meal): 5 per guest per hour

Appetizers (cocktail party only): 8 per guest per hour

Full meal menu per guest: Soup: 1 cup
Cheese: 2 ounces
Green salad: 1 ounce of greens
Vegetable sides. ½ cup
Meat and fish: 6 ounces

Thoughtful Utensils

There should be at least one serving piece per dish on the buffet. Especially with food allergies and aversions, the same utensil shouldn't be used for multiple recipes. There are so many fun options available, so look for them on sale. You can never really have too many serving spoons or pretty tongs. Scatter saucers throughout the buffet to place serving spoons down in between plates.

Keep an eye on the handles of the pieces to make sure each one is clean. As more guests move through the buffet, handles can easily be marred with salad dressings and other foods. Be prepared to swap out serving pieces for a clean one or race to wash one quickly.

Rules of the Best Buffet

Arrange the serving pieces on your buffet the night before, if possible, to make sure everything fits and looks the way you like. Make little tags to remember which platter or bowl you chose to use for which recipe. The same cards can do double duty as recipe place cards on the buffet lines to help guests in choosing exactly what they want. Here are a few tips to keep in mind when arranging your buffet:

On home buffets, it's rare to have lots of extra room that you need to fill with decorations. If so, flowers are always my first choice. A more simplistic buffet is always more appealing than one that is more crowded. Avoid random themed decorations (like Christmas ornaments on a holiday buffet) and make the food the main attraction.

Keep an eye on any spills or small cleanups that you may need to address. Everyone in the line should see as clean a buffet as the first guests.

1. At the beginning of the buffet line, arrange plates in two stacks. This is also a visual cue on where to start the line. If the buffet is on a table that is open on both sides, traffic can flow down in two lines.

2. Try to minimize guests having to reach too far when serving themselves. Everything should be easy to scoop or pick up.

3. Add place cards with the names of each dish and any good-to-know information (contains peanuts, for example).

4. Some serving pieces come with stands to elevate them a few inches. Varying height is always nice on a buffet and can save on space. Tiered stands or risers create a little extra room for plates and plates underneath. If you're using a table linen, you can stack books underneath to elevate certain dishes.

5. Place empty saucers throughout the buffet so guests have a spot to rest those messy serving spoons.

6. Any food that is the most limited should go on the end of the buffet line. Once guests' plates are almost filled, serving size will naturally be smaller.

7. Carrying separate utensils while making your way through the buffet line can be difficult so always place them at the end of the line. I love the ease and the look of flatware rolled in a napkin and placed in a basket as the last item to grab.

8. Serve drinks separate from the food if space allows. It's difficult for guests to pour a drink and manage the glass while they fix their plate on the buffet. No one knows where to safely set their glass in between platters.

Hot Food Hot and Cold Food Cold

· · · · · · · · · · · · · · · · ·

To ensure that everything served on the buffet stays safe and appetizing, don't leave any food out at room temperature for more than two hours. Keep any food for replenishing in the refrigerator (so you can swap out cold food) or in a 180°F oven to stay warm (to swap out hot food). Arranging the buffet with smaller platters and serving bowls can be helpful in keeping the freshest food possible. The smaller the vessel, the more often you will need to replenish.

I use the same system for my buffets that I do for Saturday mornings when I'm cooking homemade waffles or pancakes a few at a time. A heating pad (like your grandmother used for her back) works miracles in the kitchen. Buy one at the drug store, remove the fabric cover, and keep it in your kitchen. You'll need to hide it under a pretty kitchen towel or napkin, but it can keep things warm in a rimmed baking sheet, bread basket, or even a platter. The temperature won't heat up to a point that food safety isn't a concern, but it will keep recipes nicely warm for serving. A chafing dish is also great for heat on a buffet. If you ever see silver or vintage ones for sale, don't go home without it.

Try adding flat ice packs (that you can also buy at the drug store) under platters or bowls of cold items to hold the chill a little longer.

7

—◆—

On the Bar

It's true that when the bar runs dry, the party ends. It's the case in the South and just about everywhere else. The bar is the first place that guests will go once they arrive and quite possibly the place they visit most often during the festivities. From self-serve with a few choices to a professional on hand shaking and stirring, there is a lot of leeway on how a bar is set up. As the host, take comfort that your guests will appreciate the libations, no matter the method in which they are served.

Stocking the Bar

Always Be Ready: Red, White, and Bubbles

Wine is always around at my house and rarely would a guest be over for more than a few minutes without being offered a glass. I try to keep a few different varietals, even those that aren't our favorites, since friends may prefer something different than what Kevin and I normally pour for ourselves.

Have a couple of bottles of red, white, and sparkling at all times. If you have room, and I sincerely hope you do, keep a bottle of rosé or two within reach. Ask a guest, even if just dropping by, what they prefer and what you will be able to provide. Many homes can't spare several inches of refrigerator space to keep wines constantly chilled. If that's the case, there's an easy method of chilling wine quickly. Submerge the bottle in salty ice water, give it a spin or two, and in about 10 minutes, you have perfectly chilled wine.

Surprisingly, almost no wine is best at room temperature. They all deserve a slight cooling to be served at the optimal temperature.

Optimal Temperature for Wine
. . . .

Sparkling wines: 43°F
Dry white wines: 50°F
Medium-bodied red wines: 60°F
Full-bodied reds: 63°F

. . . .

Super-fast Chilling

Many homes can't spare several inches of refrigerator space to keep wines constantly chilled. If that's the case, there's an easy method of chilling wine quickly. Submerge the bottle in salty ice water, give it a spin or two, and in about 10 minutes, you have perfectly chilled wine.

Choosing the Perfect Wines

Don't overthink choosing wine for your party. Always serve something you have tasted and offer both a choice of at least one red and one white. Most people don't want a wine lesson on what they're about to drink at a party. So, choose wines that taste great and are approachable. Big wines like Chardonnay and Cabernet Sauvignon are less likely to be easy sipping for guests. I often go more casual and choose wines that can be enjoyed just as much without food as with it, so they tend to be less robust. These go-to grapes and regions create wines that appeal to wide audiences and are easily found in wine shops and markets. Below are some options to help get you started.

Wine Etiquette
· · · · · · · · · · ·

- Fill wine glasses about ⅓ - ½ full.

- Fill Champagne glasses about ⅔ full.

- Pour about an inch into the glass and allow the froth to settle before finishing the pour.

- Pourer lifts the glass of wine to refill, not the guest being refilled.

- Offer a clean glass when a guest is switching to a different wine.

- A stemmed glass should be held from the stem.

- Wine brought by a guest does not have to be opened. Opening is only required if the guest was asked to bring wine.

· · · · · · · · · · · · · ·

White
· · · · · ·

French Muscadet

New Zealand's
Sauvignon Blanc

Austrian dry Riesling
(If it's dry, the label will
include the term
"trocken.")

Red
· · · · ·

Pinot Noir from Oregon

Beaujolais-Villages
from France

French Côtes du Rhône

Rosé
· · ·

Choose one from
Italy, France, or
Long Island, NY

How to Open a Bottle of Bubbly

Remove the foil cover, then loosen and remove the cage. Place a kitchen towel or linen napkin over the cork. Twist the bottle, not the cork, until the cork pops out. The napkin will prevent the cork from flying away. It is thought that the less noise a cork makes on opening, the more skilled the opener is.

How to Open a Bottle of Wine

A waiter's corkscrew is the easiest way to remove a cork. Remove the foil cover. Place the corkscrew spiral (called the worm) in the center of the cork, and turn clockwise. Use the first notch of the corkscrew (called the step) onto the lip of the bottle. Use the step as leverage to pull the cork about halfway out of the bottle. The second step of the corkscrew is used to remove the cork the remainder of the way out of the bottle. If the cork breaks, remove the section that broke off and try the steps above with the remainder of the cork. If the cork can't be removed, push the cork into the bottle. Strain the wine before serving.

Southern Home Bar Echelons

No matter your budget or the size of your liquor cabinet (or bar cart or TV tray), there is a level of bar stocking that will meet your needs. If you're just starting out, begin small and add new bottles as your cocktail repertoire expands and your budget allows. The general rule I follow is to buy the best you can afford. If you haven't learned by now, opting to buy the cheapest bottle on the shelf will usually come back to haunt you and your guests the next day.

Beginner: Basically Spirited

↠ Gin
↠ Vodka
↠ Bourbon

Starting out with your first bar is exciting! Think of it as a collection that takes a while, sometimes years, to acquire as much variety as you want. And luckily, even the ones you purchase first will last. Spirits have an incredibly long shelf life. Before the bottle is opened, most alcohol will last indefinitely. Once spirits are opened, they do start to react to oxygen that will, over time, dull the flavor. Store your new bar stock in a dark and cool place (60°F is ideal), if possible. To save on all things that go with the bar, look for glassware at vintage shops and things like cocktail picks at dollar stores.

Intermediate: Well-Stocked

⇒ Gin
⇒ Vodka
⇒ Bourbon
⇒ Tequila
⇒ White Rum

When amping up your bar with a few more choices, consider sourcing them not far from home. Southern small batch distilleries are opening up in almost every state with impressive results. No matter your taste, there is likely a Southern version on the shelf—corn whiskey, gin with native botanicals, grain vodka, absinthe, liqueurs, even legit moonshine that won't land in you trouble with the law.

Advanced: Ready for Anything

- Cognac
- Gin
- Vodka
- Bourbon
- Canadian whiskey
- Rum (white and dark)
- Tequila
- Scotch
- Red and white vermouth (Store in the fridge up to two months.)
- Bitters (These help the flavors blend, but don't really add a bitter taste.)
- Cointreau

Some additional home bar accessories can take even an elite bar to a professional level. Ice freezing trays that make large cubes or balls of ice (they melt slower than smaller ones) are great for "on the rocks" drinkers. A crystal mixing glass with strainer and cocktail spoon are a gem for making one cocktail at a time. Solid wooden muddlers are pretty and bruise the leaves of herbs just enough for their flavor to be released. Sterling silver ice scoops and engraved bottle openers both round out the luxurious Southern bar.

Mixers

Mixers depend on the cocktails you plan on serving and what you like to drink. Since they don't have the shelf life and expense that alcohol does, it's easy to change them up often. Look for small bottles so leftovers don't lose fizz and have to be discarded. Use carafes, pretty bottles, or even vintage jars to spruce up mixers to a fancier level. Here are a few ideas to get you started:

- Tonic water
- Diet tonic water
- Cold filtered water
- Ice (If serving cocktails shaken and served over ice, plan on 1 pound of ice per person.)
- Ginger ale
- Cola
- Lemon-lime soda
- Juices: tomato, pineapple, cranberry, orange
- Wedges of lemons and limes
- Slices of oranges
- Olives
- Festive salt for rimming glasses

Nonalcoholic Options

No party should be held without a nonalcoholic choice at the bar. This drink needs to be just as pretty, if not more so, and inviting as any cocktail offered. The same type of glasses should be used for both nonalcoholic and every other drink. You can be as elaborate as you want with club soda, fruit juice, and sprigs of fresh herbs. Water should always be an option before the meal is served and certainly served during dinner. A meal without water on the table is one that will end in overserved guests.

Make Your Own Salt Blend
· · · · · · · · ·

Making your own salt blend for rimming glasses takes just minutes and offers a pretty finish. Try mixing kosher salt with chili powder, finely grated orange zest, or smoked paprika.

Hardware for the Bar

Mixing, Shaking, and Pouring with Charm

There's a time and a place for everything to be brand new and shiny. The bar is not it. Drink-making tools should be a collection that is eclectic and full of personality. I look for antique mallets and ice picks at estate sales and markets. Vintage cocktail picks are a real find so I like to mix and match the ones we have. Sterling silver sipping spoons have an end like a shallow spoon with a hollow handle to use like a straw. They are as long as an iced tea spoon so they work great in cocktails.

Bar Tools

- Ice bucket and pick or ice bag and mallet if you have large cubes
- Napkins
- Picks
- Stir sticks
- Muddler
- Shaker and strainer
- Jigger
- Bar spoon

"Drink-making tools should be a collection that is eclectic and full of personality."

Your grandmother's glassware is probably better quality than anything you can buy today. And, best of all, it tells a story. Don't worry if the shape of the glass isn't perfect for the drink you want to serve. I'm sure your grandmother wouldn't mind. Do be careful washing vintage glassware. If using the dishwasher, turn off the heat cycle and wash on delicate.

Glassware

A few glasses will go a long way for a home bar. Thank goodness rules have loosened up in recent years on which glass has to be used for which drink.

Wine glasses are the most versatile party glasses in your house. They work for nonalcoholic drinks, fizzy waters, wine, even cocktails are beautiful in them. If you have to start with just one set of glasses, these are your choice. Buy a standard shape, and it will work for any wine poured in it. When guests are over and fun is being had, I don't believe in stressing over a red wine glass versus a white wine glass. If storage space is an issue, stemless wine glasses are also an ideal collection for your party stash. Because they take up less room than other glasses (and can serve for a multitude of drinks), these are some of my favorites.

- Highball
- Rocks
- Martini
- Pint glasses

Remember though, whatever glasses you choose needs to work with the style of the party. If guests are holding a plate without a place to set their drink, a martini glass is going to require more concentration to keep vertical than most people drinking a martini have. I've always found them to be the most poorly designed glass.

To extend your collection, add these as you can afford or have space for them. I like to store pint glasses in the door of my freezer for the coldest beer experiences.

"Wine glasses are the most versatile party glasses in your house. They work for nonalcoholic drinks, fizzy water, wine, even cocktails."

Guessing How Much Your Guests Will Drink

There will never be an exact amount on how much your friends will drink while at your home. I've had a party in the past where we had to send a "runner" out for more liquid provisions. So, I always focus on the average and buy a little extra. How much guests consume depends on so many factors, including outside temperature, the saltiness and spiciness of the food that is being served, the time of day, the occasion, and how comfortable they are among the other guests. Here are some tips to help you plan:

Standard Bar Allowances
· ·

Wine
1 (750-milliliter) bottle of wine contains 4 (6-ounce) glasses.
Most guests will drink two glasses per hour. More white wine will
be consumed in the summer and more red wine in the winter.

Cocktails and wine
If cocktails are served before dinner and wine with
dinner, most guests will have one cocktail and possibly
three glasses of wine during dinner.

Cocktails
1.5 cocktails per guest per hour

Beer
2 beers per person per hour

Nonalcoholic
1.5 cups per guest per hour
· ·

All about Ice

Ice does the double duties of cooling cocktails as well as diluting them. Giving ice some thought is well deserved since it makes up one-third of most cocktails. The larger the piece of ice, the slower it will melt and dilute your drink. Use huge cubes for spirit-heavy drinks like a Manhattan or an Old-Fashioned. Crushed or pebble ice is ideal in fruity or frilly cocktails like a Mint Julep or Mojito. Standard cubed ice can be used for just about any drink, making it the most versatile.

Don't pull out too much ice from the freezer when tending the bar. Ice kept in the freezer will dilute a drink slower than ice that's been warmed at room temperature.

If the ice is floating in the drink, you need some more ice. The glass should have enough ice to keep it from rising to the top.

Clear ice is so very beautiful but can be very difficult to make at home. The natural gases in water freeze in the center of the ice, making it appear cloudy. To make your ice less cloudy at home, start with distilled water and set your ice trays down in a nest of kitchen towels while in the freezer.

Each shake of a cocktail shaker adds more water to your drink. Shake responsibly.

Pretty bottles of mixers and beer are totally acceptable to use as part of the bar display. Guests will know just what they are choosing and each bottle is fresh and full of bubbles. Make sure to have several bottle openers available and extra cocktail napkins to wrap around sodas and beer for condensation. As a native Georgian, Coca-Cola is a party staple at our house. I always use my grandmother's heavy-as-lead Coca-Cola cooler for ice and sodas during hot weather parties. My grandparents used it for frequent camping trips with my dad and it still stays cold like it was new.

8

In the Kitchen

My passion for entertaining started in the kitchen. I learned
to cook mainly because I hung around the kitchen looking for
snacks. It didn't take me long to learn that a girl who loves to eat
should be near the stove. Decades later, it's still a fact that I relish
feeding others. There's a connection that is made each time I cook
for someone. What better way to usher in a new friendship or
honor a lifelong relationship? Every minute that goes into hosting
a party is worth it tenfold when the first fork is raised.

Timing is Everything

The kitchen is where the magic really happens when people come over. It's the center of the timing, the tastings, the congregating, and the location of most of the fun. Keeping a running timeline is really helpful for keeping it all together. A good timeline works like a to-do list based on how far in advance duties can be done. To say I love a to-do list would be a massive understatement. I'm not ashamed that if I complete a task that wasn't on my to-do list, I write it on there just for the satisfaction of crossing it out. (Find a basic to-do list below and specific timelines for all my menus starting on page 143.)

Choosing recipes that are great reheated, or popped straight in the oven from the freezer, or those that need just a quick stir is the key to entertaining timing. Make sure that all the recipes you choose do not have last-minute needs. Know your equipment when choosing recipes. If you have a very small oven and it cooks slower than it should, plan on no more than one item that needs to be baked. All kitchens, even brand-new ones, have drawbacks and knowing them and how to work around them is crucial. If you're cooking in a kitchen that you haven't before (this happens to me often), assume nothing will work like you want it to.

Basic to-do List for Every Party
. . . .

Set up the bar

Deep-clean powder room

Choose plates and glasses

Label serving dishes

Light touch-up cleaning

Unload dishwasher

Take out the trash

. . . .

Eye on the Clock

For dinner parties, the meal needs to be served no later than one hour past the party start time. Lunch and brunch service time is no longer than 30 minutes after the start of the event.

Garden Club Lunch Timeline

- 1 Month Earlier - make tassie shells and freeze
- 2 weeks earlier - make tassie filling
- 2 days earlier - set out serving dishes, plates, napkins, etc., chill win make potato salad
- 1 day earlier - make shrimp salad and cucumber salad
- Night before - make tea
- 4 hours Earlier - last minute cleaning
- 3 hours Earlier - Run dishwasher
- 2 hours Earlier - make vinaigrette
- 1 hour earlier - unload dishwasher
- 45 minutes earlier - toast buns
- 30 minutes earlier - take out trash, add basil to tea
- 15 minutes earlier - add shrimp to buns and toss salad

Storing Silver

I store my silver in flatware chests that are lined with tarnish-resistant cloth. We also have a sideboard with a lined silver drawer (see opposite) that's perfect for pieces that we use a lot. If space doesn't allow for these specialty storage options, there are other choices that work just as well.

⇒ Storing in sealed zip-top plastic bags help to keep tarnish to a minimum.

⇒ Flannel bags made just for silver storage are inexpensive and take up very little room.

⇒ Avoid wrapping silver in plastic wrap as it can discolor silver over time.

⇒ Never use rubber bands to hold silver together because the rubber can permanently bond to the silver.

⇒ Silver should not be wrapped in newspaper.

⇒ Avoid extreme temperature storage locations, like attics and garages.

⇒ Adding a piece of chalk to where you store silver helps reduce tarnish. The chalk absorbs some of the chemicals that can cause discoloration.

Silver Stamp

Look for a stamp on sterling silver. If it's real sterling, you'll see it. Sterling is almost all pure silver with a small amount of copper mixed in for strength. Silver plate costs less than sterling because it's a coating of silver over a metal such as copper or nickel.

Other Types of Silver
. . . .

Coin Silver: Flatware that was created by melted down foreign silver currency. Because most non-domestic silver coins had varying amounts of silver content, there isn't a standard percentage of silver content.

Mexican Silver: Silver produced by Mexican and American Indian silversmiths with a minimum of 90% silver.

Silver Plated: Flatware and other objects made of a base metal before being electroplated with fine silver.

Fine Silver: Pure silver with no alloy.

. . . .

Let furniture play several roles in your house and during entertaining. My sideboard was my grandmother's and it serves to hold silver, photos I have been meaning to frame, and random earbuds from our 11-year-old. But when a party is approaching, it may turn into a dessert buffet, a stop for gathering silverware and plates, or a nice spot near the front door for guests to stand and visit.

Sterling Silver

Silver isn't necessary for entertaining; it's luxurious icing on a really good cake. Pull out your sterling or silver plate and actually enjoy all the wonderful pieces that rarely see the light of day. The best thing about silver is the more you use it, the less it tarnishes. You probably own silver that you tucked away in a felt-lined box when you married and put it up to stay safe. Take that silver out of hiding! A week or two before entertaining, set aside just a little time to make sure all your pieces of silver are in top shape.

Washing Silver with No Stress

To keep your silver in top condition throughout the year, hand wash only and dry after each use, which is the method I choose for my silver. Yes, you can put silver in the dishwasher but only if it's on the delicate cycle and there is no stainless steel touching the silver. If stainless and silver come in contact, an electrolytic reaction can occur that will pit the stainless steel. Even silver knives almost all have stainless blades, so keep them out of the dishwasher all together. Many dishwasher tubs are lined with stainless steel. All the details to take into account keep me hand washing each time.

Badly Tarnished Silver
· · · · · · · · · · · · · · · · · · · ·

Find some counter space near the sink where you can have plenty of room to work. It's best if you can also be close to a kitchen hood for ventilation or simply open a window because the smell is pretty unpleasant.

Step 1: Place the silver flatware in a disposable aluminum roasting pan set on a kitchen towel on a heatproof surface. Don't worry, you can pile them all together in the pan.

Step 2: Pour 1½ cups of baking soda on top of the silver. It will be mounded on top of the silver, and you'll think you are using too much.

Step 3: Very carefully pour boiling water over the flatware. A massive eruption of bubbles will work away the really deep tarnish. Let stand for about 5 minutes or a few minutes more, if needed.

Step 4: Remove the pieces from the hot water with tongs (the silver will be too hot to touch), rinse with cool water, and dry.

Step 5: Polish the silver with a cream silver polish. I have used Wright's Silver Cream for years. Rinse the flatware well and dry with a soft towel to prevent water spots.

For mild tarnish: Simply polish with cream silver polish, rinse, and dry with a soft towel.

· · · · · · · · · · · · · · · · · · · ·

Crystal Clear

Crystal is glass that contains minerals that can make it stronger and clearer than standard glass. The finer the crystal, the greater the clarity. For your next party, pull out the stemware you rarely use and appreciate what is probably the most elegant way to enjoy a beverage. Full-lead crystal is 24% lead and is not normally used for drinkware, but more often for decorative pieces. The crystal used for beverages has less lead content.

Caring for crystal stemware takes just a few extra steps to keep each piece in the best shape. Rinse and remove the liquids as soon as possible after use. Only hand-wash crystal in lukewarm water and dry it immediately with a lint-free cloth. The stems on glasses can pop off fairly easily during cleaning (as they are often glued on). Do not twist the bowl of the glass of the stem.

Caring for China

China is finer than everyday dishes since it's normally made of porcelain or bone china. The pieces are thinner and more delicate than a weekday plate and should be treated with more care. No one loves a dishwasher more than I do. But, when deciding if it's the right way to wash your china, consider the age. Most patterns made after 2000 will handle dishwashing fairly well. If you are using your dishwasher, opt for the gentle cycle (with no heat). Stay away from citrus detergents since the citric acid may etch the surfaces of the china. Acidic foods and coffee can stain fine china so it's best to rinse and wash those pieces as soon as possible. Arrange the pieces in the dishwasher with more space in between them than you would for your everyday dishes.

Vintage china (like your grandmother's) should be washed by hand in warm water with a mild (non-citrus) detergent. Wash as quickly after use as possible and dry right away. Especially with pieces that have been passed down to me, I take the utmost care. It's always best to be extra careful than convenient.

Storing China

The older and the more delicate the china, the more careful you should be with storing your patterns. Here are some tips:

• For plates, stack a cushioned layer in between. Felt circles or coffee filters work nicely.

• Keep china at room temperature, so avoid storing in the attic.

• Store any pieces that have lids with the lid placed upside down on the top.

• To prevent breakage, don't stack pieces too tall. Tea cups should be stacked no more than two cups high with the rim end up to prevent chipping.

Cleaning the Kitchen

Starting a party with a clean kitchen is the goal. I promise it won't stay that way! Your friends may say otherwise, but no one came over to your house to wash dishes. My guests are not allowed to help clean up in the kitchen, ever. I want them to enjoy their time at our home and relax. I'm sure they wash enough dishes at their own house. Think of the time that your friends are with you in your house as a mini-vacation for them. One way to keep them from feeling as if they need to help you clean is to not wash any dishes, not even a fork, until the door closes after the last guest. You can stack plates in the sink to keep things looking tidy, but stop there.

If you're finishing off recipes in the first few minutes of the party, you can clean your cooking utensils as you go. Make it another goal to start the party with an empty dishwasher. Cleaning up afterward then becomes fairly painless. Load the dishwasher and wipe off the counters as much as possible before you go to bed. The morning after is much more pleasant when it starts with a clean kitchen.

Friends in the Kitchen

Guests tend to congregate to the kitchen during a party. It's where everything is happening and the room where most people feel at home. Be prepared with stools at your countertop or island for them to sit and visit while you do any last-minute finishes on the meal. Set out a little snack in the kitchen so they can nibble while they catch up with the cook. I normally don't ask a guest to jump in and help in the kitchen, but if anyone asks, I always let them.

9

Guest on the Road

Graciously hosting a party is an achievement. Being a well-mannered
guest is nonnegotiable. Hosting your own parties is the best way
to learn firsthand of the importance of being a really good guest.
You become a guest the minute you receive an invitation, so your
response sets the tone as a most gracious addition to the party.
Your host has prepared for you to come over to relax, enjoy food and
drink, and spend time with friends. Conducting yourself in a way that
reflects a little of the hospitality that is being shined upon
you is a gift to your host. If there is ever any detail of attending
a party that is questioned, do what is easiest for your host.

RVSP Not Optional

You must, with absolutely no exceptions, RSVP to the host. Everyone's life is busy and time is short but it still has to be done. Letting the host know if you can come or not should be done as soon as possible from the time of receiving the invitation. Never tell the host you might be able to attend or you might drop by. Maybes are worse than not RSVPing. The only two choices are yes or no. If the response is a yes, you must attend. The host has prepared for you in time and expense, so please be respectful of that. To spare your reputation, avoid adding a "plus one" at the last minute or bringing a guest who wasn't invited. The invitation should be clear if guests are welcome. If the invitation doesn't say, look to see how the invitation was addressed. If children are welcome, the invitation should say so. If children aren't mentioned, it's generally a good rule to find a sitter.

BYOB

Accepting a request for BYOB and arriving with libations in hand has been around for decades. Those four letters are the easiest way for partygoers to know it's time to bring their own bottle. There are occasions where that is appropriate, like a cookout or tailgate, and those when it's best to leave your personal potion at home. A cocktail party or dinner party should provide all you will need.

If the host asks you to bring your own drinks, of course, do so. If she didn't ask, you're showing the host you don't trust her wine choices and bar-stocking skills. Everyone has been to parties where the wine was terrible. If it happens to you, just sip and smile.

Potluck Manners for the Guest

When attending a potluck, the host should give you an idea of which dish you should bring to the party. It may be something as simple as a "vegetable side dish" or "a chocolate dessert." If she doesn't, then ask, and keep to your assignment. Even if it's not something you love to make, stick with what the party host asked for.

Be as self-sufficient as possible when taking food to someone else's house. Any dish brought to the party should be delivered in the serving dish. Even take your own serving pieces, if possible. Arriving at a party and then asking a host for a platter creates just one more thing she has to do. Also, send a text earlier in the day if you'll need to use the oven (and at what temperature) for a quick reheat. See page 27 for tips about potluck manners as a host.

Be a Pro at Parking

Be on your best parking behavior. There's nothing like waking up the morning after a party and finding tire ruts around your driveway. When you're parking, make sure the neighbors' driveways are clear and the mailman can still get to mailboxes up and down the street.

Timing is Everything

The magic window of arrival is between on time and 15 minutes late. If you do arrive early and realize what time it is, do not get out of your car. Take time to ride around the neighborhood or do anything that will keep you from going to the door early. When you sense the party is winding down, leave. Wearing out a welcome is no one's intention.

When the host says the food is ready, either get in line at the buffet or sit down to eat. It's awkward to keep asking guests to please eat your food. I always appreciate when a friend jumps up to start the line so that other guests feel more at ease being one of the first few to eat.

Table Manners Extras

» The only items that should be around a place setting on a table are those that are needed for eating. Y'all know this, but it is not good manners to have a phone on the table at any time. If the phone needs to be nearby for babysitters that might call or for emergencies, turn it on vibrate and tuck it under your thigh or in your pocket. If you need to answer the call, excuse yourself from the table to step away.

» Try to avoid leaving lipstick on cloth napkins. If you can discreetly blot your lipstick before sitting down to the table, it will save a bit of stain-treating time for your host.

» For sit-down parties, napkins are on the table in the beginning of the meal and should not make an appearance there again. When you get up from the table for seconds or for any other reason, leave your napkin in your chair, not on the table.

» Keep your attention on those around the table and be interested in the conversation happening around you. If your closest neighbors at the table are difficult to engage with, do your best to start a conversation that includes friends farther down the table.

» If you get confused about which bread plate is yours or have a fear of drinking out of your neighbor's glass, reach under the table and form an OK sign with both of your hands. The left hand is a "b" to help you remember your bread plate is on your left. The right hand is a "d"; a clue that drink glasses are on the right of your plate.

Spills: Alert Your Host

If you spill anything at all, let the host know at once and apologize. There's no amount of apologizing that is too much to offer the host after you have a spill. Offer to help clean the spill as well as to pay for professional cleaning.

Hostess Gifts Are a Must

Never arrive at the door of a party without a little token of thanks. It doesn't need to be anything elaborate but it should be memorable. Whenever I see good hostess gifts at gift shops, I buy a few and keep them on hand so I'm never without a stash of gifts. A few of my inexpensive favorites:

⇒ Luxury soap

⇒ Nice dish towels

⇒ Outdoor insect-repellant candles

⇒ Coffee beans

⇒ Homemade preserves or pickles

Also be sure to include a little tag with your name on the gift in case you need to leave it on the counter while the hostess is busy.

Many people bring wine as a gift to a party. The hostess is not obligated to open the newly gifted bottle of wine. Most likely, wines have been chosen in advance that work with the food and the crowd. Consider the wine a gift that will be enjoyed later when the hosts have time to sit and relax in the upcoming days.

Bringing a bud vase with blooms from your yard is always appreciated. The flowers should be in a vessel that is part of the gift. Never bring flowers straight from a store to a party that the hostess has to transfer to a vase.

Sometimes you might like a more extravagant gift for a truly ample sign of appreciation. Sending flowers to the hostess the day after a party is the epitome of gratitude. There is nothing like the florist driving up on a random day.

A beautiful coffee-table book, on a subject the host is interested in, needs only a ribbon tied around it to be impressive at the door. For an evening gathering, think about gifting something that can be served for breakfast the next morning. A coffee cake or breakfast casserole (with baking instructions included) in a nonreturnable dish is about as thoughtful as it comes.

ADAIR LANG

Dear Mrs. Hardman,

Thank you for the bee box
for our garden! We hung
it where we can see it
from the window. I have
already watched four b
make their home insid
It's been so fun to ee!
You made my bir day
more special. Tha   ks for
thinking of me.

Love,
Adair

Party-Pleasing Children

When a gathering is family-friendly and children are invited, the responsibility for the children is on the parent, not the host. As a good guest, you should have well-behaved children. It's a great time for children to practice their manners and looking adults in the eye when talking. Most parties will have activities or something to occupy the little people so the adults can unwind for awhile. Just keep an eye on how yours are doing. One thing I find especially helpful when having over families is when the children all help to clean up any toys or games they used while at our house. If children are especially young, fix their plate for them. Small children and buffet lines or family-style serving often don't mix well.

Staying Overnight

Attending a party out of town often requires an overnight stay. If you're lucky, the host will offer the guest room so you can have an extra dose of hospitality. A few simple things will ensure you will be invited to stay again:

- Ask the host if you should strip the sheets off the bed before you depart.
- Make the bed when you leave (no matter if you took the sheets off or not).
- Leave a goodie for the host to find once you're gone. My sister has stayed with us countless times and still leaves a gift in the guest room.

Thank-You Notes

I wrote more thank-you notes while I was growing up than I can remember. My sister and I always had stationery and we were expected to put it to good use. I complained then, but I'm grateful now. There is no substitute for a handwritten thank-you. Emails and texts simply do not equal the charm of pen and paper. Most people now receive very few thank-you notes so the ones that arrive in the mailbox are a real treat.

No Gifts Requested
· · · · · · · · · ·
When an invitation requests no gifts, it really does mean no gifts. Do not bring one.

Keys to the Best Thank-You Notes
· ·

- Mailed within three days
- Minimum of two paragraphs with at least three sentences each
- Personal and legible handwriting
- Try to avoid stationery pre-printed with "Thank You"

· ·

10

On the Menu

The best party menus are filled with recipes that vary in flavor, colors, cooking times, and most important, are able to be mostly made ahead. My timelines will make your clock your friend and your pre-party routine a pleasant experience. Pick and choose any menu for just about any occasion and enjoy every sizzle along the way.

Bride's New Monogram Shower

It's not uncommon for a Southern closet to be half filled with monogrammed accessories and clothing. When a woman gets married, it's an undertaking to manage an all-out monogram reboot. Bring a gift with her new monogram or gift certificates to a local monogramming shop so she can pick and choose what to personalize. From jewelry, to linens, to engravings on her new sterling, the monogram possibilities are endless. Many guests, including myself, really have an aversion to themed games. Consider the invitation list before planning on adult activities.

10 a.m.

Cava-Mint-Pomegranate Sippers
Night-Before Crêpes
Rosemary Biscuits with Ham and Red-Eye Aioli
Lemoned Asparagus
Spinach Berry Salad with Pumpkin Seeds
Rocky Road Brownies

Timeline

1 to 2 Days Earlier
- Make Red-Eye Aioli. Cover and refrigerate.
- Make crêpes. Store in a large ziplock bag with wax paper between each one.
- Chill any wine to be served.
- Set out napkins and all serving dishes with labels, plates, utensils, and glasses.

1 Day Earlier
- Make brownies. Cool; do not cut into squares. Cover pan with foil.
- Make asparagus. Cover and refrigerate.
- Make dressing for salad. Cover and store at room temperature.
- Slice onion for salad. Store in a ziplock plastic bag in the refrigerator.
- Slice fruit for the bar.

Night Before
- Mix pomegranate juice and honey for the sippers. Chill overnight.
- Slice lemons, store in a ziplock plastic bag in the refrigerator.
- Make biscuits. Cool and store in a large ziplock plastic bag at room temperature.

4 Hours Earlier
- Zip around for last-minute cleaning.

3 Hours Earlier
- Run the dishwasher for the last time before guests arrive.

2 Hours Earlier
- Cut the brownies into squares.

1 Hour Earlier
- Unload any clean dishes from dishwasher.
- Cut romaine hearts into quarters for salad. Cover with a damp paper towel.

45 Minutes Earlier
- Arrange mint and pomegranate seeds in Champagne glasses.
- Preheat oven to 300°F to reheat biscuits.

30 Minutes Earlier
- Wrap biscuits in foil; reheat in the oven for 5 minutes. Assemble biscuits.
- Assemble salad, leaving dressing on side.
- Take out the trash.

15 Minutes Earlier
- Stir Cava and lemons into sippers. Pour into glasses when serving.
- Reheat crêpes in the microwave for 20 to 30 seconds each.
- Add zest and mint to asparagus.

Night-Before Crêpes

Crêpes tend to be off the table for morning parties because they are last minute to make. Thanks to a few extra eggs in the batter, this herb-filled version can be made ahead and easily reheated before serving.

serves 8

8 large eggs

1½ cups all-purpose flour

1¾ cups half-and-half

4 tablespoons unsalted butter, melted

1 teaspoon table salt

¼ cup chopped fresh flat-leaf parsley

¼ cup chopped fresh dill

Cooking spray

Sour cream

1. Process the first 5 ingredients in a blender until smooth. Add the parsley and dill; pulse to combine.

2. Heat a 10-inch nonstick skillet coated with cooking spray over medium. Pour about a scant ⅓ cup of the batter into pan; quickly tilt in all directions so the batter covers the bottom of pan evenly. Cook 1 to 2 minutes or until the crêpe is set and can be shaken loose from pan. Turn the crêpe; cook 30 seconds. Repeat with remaining batter, stirring the batter occasionally to disperse herbs and coating the pan with cooking spray between each crêpe.

3. Allow the crêpes to cool slightly. Stack the crêpes with wax paper in between each one. Place in a large ziplock plastic bag and refrigerate overnight. To serve, remove from wax paper and reheat crêpes in microwave 20 to 30 seconds. Fold into quarters, with herbed side out, and place on a serving platter. Serve the crêpes with the sour cream. This yields 16 crêpes.

.

Cava-Mint-Pomegranate Sippers

I have had a love for anything with bubbles my entire adult life. If you come to my house, your chances of a sparkly drink are pretty good. Most recipes call for making bubbly cocktail by the glass and that can be time-consuming. Making a batch in a pitcher and giving yourself a small window to chill makes life easier. Combine the juice and honey in the pitcher in advance and just add the other ingredients before serving. Nothing made with bubbles should ever cause any stress.

serves 8

1½ cups pomegranate juice

¼ cup honey

2 (750-milliliter) bottles chilled Cava

1 lemon, sliced

2 tablespoons pomegranate seeds

Fresh mint sprigs

1. Combine the juice and honey in a pitcher, stirring until the honey dissolves. Add the Cava and sliced lemons. This yields 7¾ cups. Chill until ready to serve (but no more than 30 minutes so bubbles hang around).

2. In the Champagne glasses, divide the pomegranate seeds and a sprig of mint. Top with the Cava mixture, and serve immediately.

Lemoned Asparagus

Serving asparagus on a buffet is a great way to add color and is an ideal make-ahead vegetable. I prefer the skinnier spears of asparagus, but feel free to choose whatever size you like. If you're making ahead, toss the asparagus in the lemon mixture and chill for up to one day. Add the zest and mint right before serving.

serves 8

3 pounds asparagus

3 lemons

2 tablespoons apple cider vinegar

½ tablespoon sorghum syrup

½ teaspoon Dijon mustard

¼ teaspoon table salt

⅛ teaspoon freshly ground black pepper

¼ cup olive oil

Garnish: fresh mint

1. Trim the tough ends off each asparagus spear. Bring a large pot of water to a boil. Add the asparagus; cook for 3 minutes or until tender-crisp. Drain and rinse in very cold water. Pat dry.

2. Zest the lemon with a strip zester to make little ribbons of peel.

3. Juice the lemons after zesting. Whisk together 3 tablespoons lemon juice, vinegar, and the next 4 ingredients. Slowly add the olive oil in a steady stream while whisking constantly.

4. Arrange the asparagus on a deep platter, and pour the lemon mixture over the spears. Gently roll the spears to coat. Top the asparagus with the reserved lemon zest and mint before serving.

Rosemary Biscuits with Ham and Red-Eye Aioli

I've always liked ham in biscuits but I amped it up with a little instant coffee to give them a taste reminiscent of red-eye gravy. Guests always appreciate homemade biscuits. Get dirty in the flour and bask in the heat of the oven. It's worth it. Make the aioli a day or two in advance and the biscuits the day before. They reheat fine in the oven wrapped in foil for a few minutes.

serves 8

2 cups self-rising soft-wheat flour (such as White Lily)

¼ cup vegetable shortening

1 teaspoon finely chopped fresh rosemary

⅔ cup whole buttermilk

⅓ cup heavy cream

Red-Eye Aioli

¼ pound thinly sliced sweet ham

1. Preheat the oven to 450°F. Place a 10-inch skillet in the oven while preheating.

2. Place the flour in a large bowl. Add the shortening, and use a pinching motion with your fingers to break it up and work it into the flour. The flour will look more like crumbs. Stir in the rosemary. Add the buttermilk and cream, stirring just until the mixture is wet and looks messy.

3. Turn the dough out onto a lightly floured counter. Using floured hands, knead the dough 4 or 5 times by folding dough over and pressing down with the heels of your hands to make a smooth dough. (The dough should not be sticky.)

4. Pat the dough to ¾-inch thickness. Cut 16 biscuits with a 2-inch round cutter. (Be very careful not to twist the cutter so the biscuits won't be lopsided.) Combine any dough scraps, pat to ¾-inch thickness, and cut into rounds (discard any remaining scraps). Place the biscuits, with the sides touching each other, in hot skillet.

5. Bake at 450°F for 16 minutes or until lightly browned. Cool slightly.

6. Cut the biscuits in half and spread the Red-Eye Aioli on each half. Stuff each biscuit with a folded piece of ham. Serve warm or at room temperature.

Red-Eye Aioli

¼ cup mayonnaise

½ teaspoon instant espresso coffee (I use Café Bustelo)

½ teaspoon apple cider vinegar

3 dashes of hot sauce

Stir together all the ingredients. Cover and chill for up to 3 days.

Spinach Berry Salad with Pumpkin Seeds

I always like to have a salad during a brunch, but I want it to be very colorful and slightly sweet. The overload of berries with baby spinach fits the bill perfectly. The dressing can be made ahead. Assemble the salad just before serving.

serves 8

1 (5-ounce) container baby spinach

6 ounces raspberries (about 1 cup)

6 ounces blueberries (about 1 cup)

⅓ cup thinly sliced red onion (from 1 small)

¼ cup roasted pumpkin seeds (pepitas)

¼ cup olive oil

2 tablespoons apple cider vinegar

1 tablespoon honey

¼ teaspoon table salt

¼ teaspoon freshly ground black pepper

1. Combine the spinach and next 4 ingredients in a serving bowl.

2. Whisk together the olive oil and next 4 ingredients. Serve the dressing on the side.

Rocky Road Brownies

These brownies have all of my favorite treats in each bite: fudgy frosting, rich pecans, and sweet marshmallows. Make them the day before the party. Wait to cut them until closer to serving time to make sure each square stays moist. Finish off each serving with a monogram pick in honor of the bride.

serves 10 to 12

1 cup coarsely chopped pecans

¾ cup salted butter

2 ounces unsweetened chocolate
  baking bar, chopped

2 cups granulated sugar

4 large eggs

1 cup all-purpose flour

¼ cup unsweetened cocoa

1 tablespoon espresso-ground coffee

⅛ teaspoon table salt

1 teaspoon vanilla extract

2 cups miniature marshmallows

Chocolate Frosting

1. Preheat the oven to 350°F. Toast pecans in a single layer in a shallow pan 6 to 8 minutes or until lightly toasted and fragrant.

2. Combine butter and chopped chocolate in a medium saucepan. Cook over medium-low heat, stirring constantly, 4 minutes or until melted. Remove from heat.

3. Whisk in the sugar and eggs until well blended. Combine the flour, cocoa, coffee, and salt. Stir into the flour mixture until blended. Add vanilla. Fold in marshmallows. Lightly grease a 13- x 9-inch pan. Line the bottom and sides with foil, allowing 2 to 3 inches to extend over sides; lightly grease foil. Spread the batter into pan.

4. Bake in the preheated oven for 25 to 30 minutes or until a wooden pick inserted in center comes out with a few moist crumbs. Sprinkle the warm brownies with the toasted pecans and marshmallows.

5. Prepare Chocolate Frosting. Pour over the pecans and marshmallows; spread to edges. Spreading over the bumpy pecans and marshmallows will feel like you're doing it wrong, but you're not. Let cool 1 hour on a wire rack. Cut into 24 squares.

Chocolate Frosting

½ cup salted butter

⅓ cup milk

6 tablespoons unsweetened cocoa

1 (16-ounce) package powdered sugar
  (3½ cups)

1 teaspoon vanilla extract

Combine the first 3 ingredients in a large saucepan. Stir constantly over medium heat just until the butter melts, 4 to 5 minutes. Remove from heat. Use a handheld electric mixer to beat in the powdered sugar and vanilla in the warm saucepan until smooth. Use immediately. Makes 2 cups.

Bloody Mary Brunch

If I had to choose my favorite time of day to entertain, it would be in the morning for several reasons. I could live on breakfast foods, it's usually less expensive than parties in the evening, and it allows for an after-party nap before sundown. Kevin and I got married in the morning mainly for the excuse of having bacon and biscuits at the reception.

Recipes that can be made the day before are essential for a brunch menu that works. If you get up in the middle of the night to cook for the morning, the life of the party certainly won't be you.

11 a.m.

Homemade Red-Eye Bloody Mary Bar

Make-Ahead Cinnamon Coffee Cake

Ruby Red Ambrosia

Brussels Sprouts with Apples and Bacon Vinaigrette

Charleston Shrimp and Cream Cheese Grits

Timeline

1 to 2 Days Earlier
- Set out all serving dishes with labels, plates, utensils, pitchers, carafes, and glasses.
- Set out napkins.
- Chill any wine to be served.

1 Day Earlier
- Make Charleston Shrimp (not Cream Cheese Grits). Cover tightly and refrigerate.
- Slice Brussels sprouts. Seal in a ziplock plastic bag and refrigerate.
- Cook bacon for salad; refrigerate separately from reserved drippings.
- Make ambrosia. Cover and refrigerate.
- Slice fruit for the bar.

Night Before
- Prepare garnishes in serving bowls for Bloody Mary bar. Cover and refrigerate.
- Assemble coffee cake batter. Cover and refrigerate.
- Make Nut Crumble; refrigerate until morning.

4 Hours Earlier
- Zip around for last-minute cleaning in the house.

3 Hours Earlier
- Stir together Bloody Mary mixture; chill in refrigerator until serving.
- Run the dishwasher for the last time before guests arrive.

2 Hours Earlier
- Assemble Bacon Vinaigrette.

1 Hour Earlier
- Unload any clean dishes from dishwasher.
- Make Cream Cheese Grits. Keep warm on low heat until serving, stirring occasionally.

45 Minutes Earlier
- Toss together Brussels Sprouts with Apples and Bacon Vinaigrette.

30 Minutes Earlier
- Reheat Charleston Shrimp on low heat until bubbly, stirring occasionally.
- Assemble salad, leaving dressing on side.
- Take out the trash.

15 Minutes Earlier
- Make Drizzle Icing for the coffee cake.

Homemade Red-Eye Bloody Mary Bar

It's always morning somewhere, right? There's no need to turn to bottled mixes when you can wow your guests with your own and throw in a touch of caffeine for a boost. Choosing organic tomato juice adds a bright flavor that I really like. Look for it next to the bottles of standard tomato juice. I also think juice in plastic or glass containers tastes much better than those sold in metal cans. Mixing all the ingredients in advance in one pitcher makes for easy serving for a thirsty crowd. Set up the garnishes and let everyone personalize their own.

serves 8

32 ounces organic tomato juice (4 cups)

¼ cup fresh lemon juice (from 1 large lemon)

¼ cup fresh lime juice (from 2 medium limes)

¼ cup prepared horseradish

¼ cup pickled jalapeño brine

2 tablespoons Worcestershire sauce

1 teaspoon hot sauce

1 teaspoon instant espresso coffee (I use Café Bustelo)

1½ cups good vodka

Old Bay seasoning (mixed with kosher salt for rimming the glasses)

Hot sauce

Lime wedges

Lemon wedges

Olives

Celery sticks with leaves attached

Pepperoncini peppers

Pickled okra

Fresh rosemary sprigs

Stir together the tomato juice and next 7 ingredients in a pitcher. Slowly whisk in the vodka. This yields 6½ cups. Chill the mixture for at least 1 hour. Stir well before serving so everyone gets their fair share of the hard stuff. Serve over ice with the hot sauce and garnishes.

Make-Ahead Cinnamon Coffee Cake

No brunch should take place without a coffee cake. Serving a warm cake in the morning often means getting up before the sun, but letting the batter chill overnight keeps the early alarm silent. Because the batter rests in the baking pan, there's no pressure to perform a dive into the bakeware cabinet before enjoying the first cup of coffee.

serves 8 to 10

¾ cup unsalted butter, softened

½ cup granulated sugar

½ cup firmly packed light brown sugar

2 large eggs

2 cups all-purpose flour

1 teaspoon baking powder

1 teaspoon baking soda

½ teaspoon table salt

¼ teaspoon ground cinnamon

1 cup sour cream

⅓ cup heavy cream

1 teaspoon vanilla extract

Nut Crumble

Drizzle Icing

1. Beat the butter in the bowl of an electric mixer at medium speed until creamy; gradually add the sugars, beating well. Add the eggs, 1 at a time, beating just until blended after each addition.

2. Combine the flour and next 4 ingredients in a medium bowl. Combine sour cream and next 2 ingredients together in a small bowl. With the mixer on low speed, add the flour mixture to the butter mixture alternately with the sour cream mixture, beginning and ending with the flour. Allow each addition to be fully incorporated before continuing. Pour the batter into a greased and floured 13- x 9-inch pan. Cover tightly, and chill 8 to 24 hours.

3. Preheat the oven to 350°F. Let the batter stand at room temperature 30 minutes. Sprinkle with the Nut Crumble. Bake in the preheated oven 32 to 35 minutes or until a wooden pick inserted in center comes out clean. Pour the Drizzle Icing over the cake.

Nut Crumble

While the chilled batter comes to room temperature, stir together ¾ cup coarsely chopped pecans, ¾ cup sliced almonds, ½ cup firmly packed light brown sugar, 6 tablespoons all-purpose flour, ¼ cup melted butter, and ½ teaspoon ground cinnamon. Makes 2 cups.

Drizzle Icing

Stir together 1 cup powdered sugar and 2 tablespoons milk until glossy and looks like satin ribbons when a spoon is lifted from the bowl. Makes about 1 cup.

Ruby Red Ambrosia

Ambrosia has been on party menus for ages. We always had it dressed up with maraschino cherries on Christmas mornings. I've brightened the flavor and enlivened the color with red grapefruit. If red grapefruit is hard to find, pink will work just fine. Adding Meyer lemon juice adds another layer of citrus without being too sour. Ambrosia can be made one day in advance and chilled until serving.

serves 8

10 pounds Ruby Red grapefruit, peeled and segmented (6½ cups segments)

3 navel oranges, peeled and segmented (1½ cups segments)

⅔ cup sweetened flaked coconut

¼ cup Meyer lemon juice (1 lemon)

3 tablespoons honey

⅛ teaspoon table salt

Garnish: fresh mint

1. Combine the grapefruit, oranges, and coconut in a serving bowl.

2. Whisk together the lemon juice, honey, and salt. Stir into the grapefruit mixture. This yields 8 cups. Garnish with the mint. Serve with a slotted spoon.

Brussels Sprouts with Apples and Bacon Vinaigrette

This hearty salad is best put together right before serving, but almost all the ingredients can be prepped ahead so the only thing left for the last minute is stirring. To make a vegetarian version, simply use olive oil instead of bacon drippings in the dressing, and adjust the salt as you like.

serves 8

½ pound thick-sliced bacon (8 slices), chopped

2 shallots, diced (about ⅓ cup)

⅓ cup apple cider vinegar

2 pounds Brussels sprouts

1 cup loosely packed fresh flat-leaf parsley, chopped

1 Gala apple, diced (about 1 cup)

Pomegranate seeds (about 1 cup)

2 tablespoons olive oil

2 teaspoons light brown sugar

1 teaspoon Dijon mustard

½ teaspoon table salt

½ teaspoon freshly ground black pepper

1. Cook the bacon in a large skillet over medium-low for 15 minutes or until crispy. Using a slotted spoon, remove the bacon, reserving the drippings in the skillet. Drain the bacon on paper towels, and set aside. (You should have about ½ cup bacon drippings. If you have less, add extra olive oil.)

2. Combine the shallots and vinegar and let stand for 15 minutes.

3. Remove the outer leaves and stems from the Brussels sprouts, and cut in half lengthwise, then cut into ¼-inch slices. Combine the Brussels sprouts and next 3 ingredients in a large serving bowl.

4. Whisk together the reserved bacon drippings, shallot mixture, olive oil, brown sugar, Dijon mustard, salt, and pepper.

5. Toss together the Brussels sprouts with the dressing and reserved cooked bacon.

Charleston Shrimp and Cream Cheese Grits

I fell in love with shrimp and grits while in culinary school in Charleston, South Carolina. Different variations are at nearly every restaurant, and I tried my best to eat them all before graduation. I am biased, but believe me, this recipe is at the top of the top. I've been asked to make this at holiday gatherings more than anything else. My family likes the green hot pepper sauce from Tabasco, but using a hotter red variety is good too. Don't wince at using quick grits. There is so much going on in this recipe, you can get away with it. They are deceiving in that they really aren't as quick as they say. I normally cook them for about 30 minutes to achieve the creaminess I like. If you use stone ground, just count on more cooking time. The shrimp can be made a day in advance and the flavors get even better overnight. The grits are best made the day of the party.

serves 8

1 (12-ounce) package bacon (8 slices), chopped

2 tablespoons unsalted butter

1 large onion, chopped

1 medium-size red bell pepper, chopped

3 garlic cloves, minced

⅓ cup all-purpose flour

3 cups chicken broth

1 tablespoon Worcestershire sauce

Juice of 1 lemon (about 2 tablespoons)

2½ pounds medium peeled, deveined raw shrimp

1½ tablespoons chopped fresh thyme

1 tablespoon chopped fresh flat-leaf parsley

¼ teaspoon table salt

¼ teaspoon freshly ground black pepper

Cream Cheese Grits

Hot sauce, to taste

1. Cook the chopped bacon in a large Dutch oven over medium until browned and crispy, about 15 minutes, stirring frequently. Remove the bacon to paper towels to drain, reserving the drippings in the pan. Set aside the cooked bacon. Add the butter to the drippings, whisking until melted.

2. Once the butter is melted, add the onion, bell pepper, and garlic to the bacon drippings mixture, and cook over medium until softened, about 5 minutes. Sprinkle the flour over the onion mixture. Cook for 2 minutes, stirring constantly. Slowly pour in the chicken broth and next 2 ingredients. Bring to a boil, reduce heat, and simmer over medium-low, uncovered, for 20 minutes.

3. Add the shrimp, thyme, and parsley, and cook for 3 to 4 minutes, stirring occasionally. (The shrimp will be pink and curled, and the sauce thickened.) Add the salt and pepper. Serve the shrimp over the Cream Cheese Grits, and sprinkle with the reserved crumbled bacon and hot sauce.

Cream Cheese Grits

6 cups chicken broth

1 cup uncooked quick-cooking grits
(not instant)

1 (8-ounce) package cream cheese, at
room temperature

Bring chicken broth and grits to a simmer in a large saucepan. Cook, whisking very often, for 30 minutes or until the grits are no longer crunchy. (The only way to tell if grits are done is to taste for texture.) Add the cream cheese to the grits, and stir until melted and well blended.

Garden Club Lunch

Some the South's most magnificent gardens exist due to members of garden clubs all over the country. Not only do most garden club members take pleasure in getting out in the yard to plant and pull weeds, they also work diligently to save native plants, historic gardens, and educate the public on the benefits we all receive from the plants around us. I have been a member of Junior Ladies Garden Club (a Garden Club of America member club) in Athens for years. All of that work, in and out of the soil, can work up an appetite for a cheerful ladies' luncheon filled with fellowship and good food.

Noon
. . . . .

Pineapple Basil Tea

Arugula Salad with Pepper Jelly Vinaigrette

Cucumber, Kalamata, and Tomato Salad

Creamy Red Potato Salad

Georgia Shrimp Rolls

Key Lime Tassies

Timeline
. . . .

1 Month Earlier
- Make tart shells for tassies, and freeze them unfilled in a large ziplock plastic freezer bag.

2 Weeks Earlier
- Make Key lime filling for tassies. Store, covered, in refrigerator.

1 to 2 Days Earlier
- Set out all serving dishes with labels, plates, utensils, pitchers, and glasses.
- Set out napkins.
- Make potato salad, cover, and chill until serving.
- Chill any wine to be served.

1 Day Earlier
- Make shrimp salad for rolls. Store in a large ziplock bag in the refrigerator.
- Make cucumber salad. Cover and store in the refrigerator.
- Slice fruit for the bar.

Night Before
- Make the tea ahead, up until it's time to add the basil. Chill overnight.

4 Hours Earlier
- Zip around for last-minute cleaning in the house.

3 Hours Earlier
- Run the dishwasher for the last time before guests arrive.

2 Hours Earlier
- Make Pepper Jelly Vinaigrette. Store at room temperature

1 Hour Earlier
- Unload any clean dishes from dishwasher.

45 Minutes Earlier
- Toast hot dog buns for shrimp rolls.

30 Minutes Earlier
- Take out the trash.
- Stir basil and water into tea.

15 Minutes Earlier
- Fill buns with shrimp.
- Toss salad, and top with cheese.

Georgia Shrimp Rolls

On a girls' trip to Martha's Vineyard, I fell in love with lobster rolls. My friend Jennifer Jaax and I took off on a journey on bicycles to find the island's best rolls. We heard they were served at a church right on the water as a fund-raiser. We sat in the grass and ate them beside our kickstands. With Georgia shrimp close by nearly all the time, I like making the standard Northern favorite with a Southern spin. It always reminds me I need to take girls' trips more often! Shrimp aren't as meaty as lobster, but they make this recipe much less expensive and more local. Buying pre-cooked wild shrimp at the seafood market makes this recipe incredibly easy. Make sure to use top-sliced hot dog buns for a touch of authenticity. You can make the shrimp salad one day in advance.

serves 8

⅓ cup diced sweet onion

2 tablespoons fresh lemon juice

1½ pounds cooked medium shrimp (with tails on) or 1¼ pounds cooked shrimp without tails

¼ cup diced celery

¼ cup mayonnaise

½ teaspoon table salt

¼ teaspoon freshly ground black pepper

3 tablespoons chopped fresh flat-leaf parsley

¼ cup unsalted butter, softened

8 top-sliced hot dog buns

1. Combine sweet onion and lemon juice. Let sit for 20 minutes.

2. If shrimp have tails, remove them and discard. Cut shrimp in half so they will be bite-sized. Combine shrimp, onion and lemon juice mixture, and next 5 ingredients in a mixing bowl. Cover and chill while buns are toasting.

3. Spread butter on sides and bottom of hot dog buns. Toast outside of buns in a non-stick skillet or griddle, in batches if needed, over medium-low heat until browned. Remove buns from heat and stuff a heaping ⅓ cup shrimp mixture into each. Serve immediately.

Pineapple Basil Tea

Sweet tea is so common around the South, it's nice to dress it up and try new kinds of tea when friends come over. Green tea is one of my absolute favorites. Pineapples are a famous symbol of hospitality and the quintessential flavor addition to a Southern lunch. The juice makes the tea sweet, but not too sweet. Look for fresh pineapple juice from a local juice bar or jarred organic pure pineapple juice not from concentrate.

serves 8

7 cups water

8 green tea bags or ½ cup loose green tea

½ cup granulated sugar

1 cup pineapple juice

¼ cup fresh basil leaves, gently torn

1. Bring water to a boil in a medium saucepan. Remove from heat and add the tea bags. Steep 5 minutes. Discard the tea bags, and add the sugar, stirring until fully dissolved.

2. Stir in pineapple juice. Allow to cool.

3. Stir in basil right before serving. Pour over ice.

Arugula Salad with Pepper Jelly Vinaigrette

Homemade pepper jelly often arrives on my front porch from my friend Crystal Leach, who makes the world's best spicy-sweet concoction. Her peppers seem to float effortlessly throughout the jar. If you don't have friends this good, you can find some good brands available in grocery stores as well. This salad is a great example of all that can be done with the famous Southern jelly other than slather it on cream cheese. Make the dressing a few hours ahead, and just toss the salad right before serving.

serves 8

¼ cup pepper jelly

2 tablespoons white wine vinegar

1 teaspoon Dijon mustard

¼ teaspoon table salt

⅛ teaspoon freshly ground black pepper

2 tablespoons olive oil

5 ounces baby arugula (5 cups)

⅓ cup toasted pecans, roughly chopped

Garnish: 2 ounces crumbled goat cheese
 (½ cup)

1. Heat the pepper jelly in a small saucepan over low for about 2 minutes or until melted. Allow to cool.

2. Combine the jelly and next 4 ingredients in a 2-cup glass measuring cup. Slowly add the olive oil in a steady stream, whisking constantly. (To make sure the measuring cup stays still on the counter while whisking with one hand and pouring with the other, set it on a wet paper towel.) This yields ⅓ cup dressing.

3. Combine the arugula and pecans in a bowl; pour the dressing over the salad, and toss to coat. Arrange the salad on a platter, and garnish with the crumbled goat cheese. Serve immediately.

Cucumber, Kalamata, and Tomato Salad

This salad always reminds me of all the best a Southern vegetable garden can offer. It's super-easy for a crowd and is even better when made ahead. Olives add a briny flavor to this already zesty dressing that's bursting with summer flavor and crunch. Make the salad up to a day ahead. The flavors just get better each hour.

serves 12

3 large seedless cucumbers, chopped

3 small red and yellow tomatoes, sliced

1 small red onion, sliced into half moons

1 cup kalamata olives, pitted and cut
  in half

⅓ cup olive oil

¼ cup red wine vinegar

½ teaspoon table salt

¼ teaspoon freshly ground black pepper

⅓ cup crumbled feta cheese

1. Combine the cucumbers and next 3 ingredients in a serving bowl.

2. Whisk together the oil and next 3 ingredients; pour over the cucumber mixture, and toss to coat. Cover and chill at least 2 hours. Top with the feta cheese before serving. This yields 12 cups.

Creamy Red Potato Salad

Replacing some of the mayonnaise with sour cream in this potato salad lends a slightly tangy taste and feels lighter than the traditional versions. I like to use red potatoes because the color of the skin makes the prettiest salad. Make the entire salad ahead of time and chill until serving.

serves 8

3 pounds red potatoes

½ cup sour cream

½ cup mayonnaise

Zest of 1 lemon

2 tablespoons white vinegar

1 teaspoon table salt

¼ teaspoon freshly ground black pepper

⅔ cup sliced scallions

1. Cover the potatoes with cold water. Bring to a boil in a large saucepan over medium-high, reduce the heat to medium-low, and cook for 20 minutes or until they are tender when stuck with a fork. Let cool; cut into 1-inch pieces.

2. Combine the sour cream and next 5 ingredients in a large bowl. Add the potatoes and scallions, and toss to coat. Cover and chill 1 hour before serving or up to 2 days.

Key Lime Tassies

Serving something mini for dessert is nice during the day when guests may be ready to mill about in the warm sunshine. Homemade crust and Key lime curd are impressive, but shockingly make-ahead friendly. The filling can be made up to two weeks in advance and the baked shells can be frozen up to a month. Just thaw at room temperature and fill the shells before the party. Expect a little extra lime curd. Spread it on pound cake or fruit or on a spoon so nothing goes to waste.

makes about 48 tassies

Key Lime Curd

2 cups granulated sugar

½ cup unsalted butter, softened

4 large eggs, at room temperature

1 cup freshly squeezed or bottled Key
  lime juice, such as Nellie & Joe's, at
  room temperature

Almond Cream Cheese Pastry

1 cup sliced almonds

2¾ cups all-purpose flour

1 (8-ounce) package cream cheese,
  at room temperature

1 cup unsalted butter, softened

¼ cup granulated sugar

Garnish: whipped cream, thinly sliced
  limes (optional)

1. Prepare the Key Lime Curd: Beat 2 cups sugar and ½ cup butter in the bowl of an electric stand mixer on medium speed until blended. Add the eggs, 1 at a time, beating just until blended after each addition. Gradually add the Key lime juice to the butter mixture, beating on low speed just until blended after each addition. (Don't worry if it looks like it's separating. It will come together once it's heated and whisked.)

2. Transfer the mixture to a heavy 4-quart saucepan. Cook over medium-low, whisking constantly, until the mixture thickens and just begins to bubble, 14 to 16 minutes. Remove the saucepan from the heat, and allow to cool for 30 minutes. Place plastic wrap directly on surface (to prevent a film from forming), and chill until firm, about 4 hours. Refrigerate in an airtight container up to 2 weeks.

3. Prepare the Almond Cream Cheese Pastry: Process almonds in a blender or food processor until finely ground. Combine ground almonds and flour. Beat the cream cheese, 1 cup butter, and ¼ cup sugar in the bowl of an electric stand mixer on medium speed until creamy. Gradually add the almond and flour mixture to the butter mixture, beating on low speed just until blended. Use a small cookie scoop (1 ⅝ inch-diameter) to make about 48 scoops of dough. Shape each scoop into a ball. To make ahead, wrap rolled dough tightly in plastic and freeze for up to 1 month. Let soften before pressing into muffin pans.

continued

4. Preheat the oven to 400°F. Place 1 dough ball into each cup of lightly greased miniature muffin pans; press the dough into bottoms and up sides of cups, forming shells. Chill dough in pans for 10 minutes.

5. Bake in the preheated oven until lightly browned, about 14 minutes. Remove the shells from pans to wire racks, and cool completely, about 20 minutes.

6. Spoon 1 heaping teaspoon of the curd into each pastry shell. Store the tassies in a container with a lid that won't touch the top of the tassies so the curd won't get scuffed. Chill until ready to serve. Just before serving, dollop the filled shells evenly with the whipped cream and, if desired, garnish with the lime slices.

Tassie Shells to the Rescue

Keeping tassie shells in the freezer for unexpected guests is an easy way to stay ready. The slightly sweet pastry works well with almost any dessert filling. Try a little scoop of fig preserves and a touch of whipped cream, a dollop of crème fraîche and a plump raspberry, or mascarpone with a drizzle of honey and a few blueberries. If a lemon craving hits, just replace the lime juice with lemon in the curd recipe.

Funeral Reception

Having a gathering of mourners to a home after a funeral is a Southern tradition. If you host one properly, like our mothers and grandmothers did, you pull out every piece of china, crystal, and silver that you can. Women in the South have been known to start polishing their silver when a death is imminent or when one has just occurred. It's therapeutic and is probably necessary.

Midday
(depending on the time of the funeral, of course)
. . . . . .

Old-Fashioned Pecan Cheese Ball

Lemon-Shallot Green Beans

Buttermilk Yeast Rolls   Squash Casserole

Roasted Beef Tenderloin with Creamy Horseradish Sauce and Vidalia Onion Chimichurri

Just Chess Pie

Timeline
. . . .

1 Month Earlier (or to keep in the freezer since a long lead time doesn't occur here)
- Make yeast rolls, and cool. Wrap in foil, and place in a large ziplock plastic freezer bag. Freeze.

1 to 2 Days Earlier
- Set out all serving dishes with labels, plates, utensils, and glasses. Set out napkins.
- Make chimichurri and horseradish sauces. Cover and refrigerate.
- Make cheese ball. Wrap in wax paper, and store in a ziplock plastic bag in the refrigerator.
- Chill wine, beer, and mixers to be served.
- Set up bar with glasses, ice bucket, and other hardware needed.

1 Day Earlier
- Make chess pie, and store at room temperature.

- Blanch green beans. Store in a large ziplock plastic bag in the refrigerator.
- Mince garlic and slice shallots for beans. Store in a ziplock plastic bag in the refrigerator.
- Cook beef tenderloin, and slice. Store in a ziplock plastic bag in the refrigerator.
- Slice fruit for the bar.

Night Before
- Assemble squash casserole, without cracker topping, and refrigerate.

4 Hours Earlier
- Zip around for last-minute cleaning.

3 Hours Earlier
- Run the dishwasher for the last time before guests arrive.

2 Hours Earlier
- Preheat oven to 350°F for baking squash casserole and reheating rolls.

1 Hour Earlier
- Unload clean dishes from dishwasher.
- Add the crackers to the squash casserole, and bake for 35 minutes.
- Let chimichurri and horseradish sauces come to room temperature.

45 Minutes Earlier
- Finish off green beans with garlic and shallots in a skillet.

30 Minutes Earlier
- Take out the trash.
- Heat rolls, still wrapped in foil, for about 25 minutes.
- Set out cheese ball to soften slightly.

15 Minutes Earlier
- Set out beef tenderloin slices to come to room temperature.

Old-Fashioned Pecan Cheese Ball

Ask just about any Southerner and they have a cheese ball story. My grandmother made a cheese ball for every holiday. When assignments were made as to who would make what, she always got the job of the cheese ball. I like to divide the cheese to make two smaller versions so it's easy to replenish at a party quickly and easily. A half-eaten cheese ball isn't pretty. Check this recipe off your list early. It's great made days in advance.

serves 8 to 10

1 (8-ounce) package cream cheese, at room temperature

4 ounces sharp Cheddar cheese, shredded (1 cup)

1 tablespoon drained, finely chopped pimiento

2 teaspoons finely chopped flat-leaf parsley

2 tablespoons minced shallot

1 teaspoon Worcestershire sauce

1 teaspoon lemon zest

Dash of cayenne pepper

⅛ teaspoon table salt

¾ cup finely chopped toasted pecans

Assorted crackers

1. Beat the cream cheese and the next 8 ingredients with an electric mixer at medium speed until combined and creamy. Divide the cheese mixture in half, and shape each half into a ball.

2. Coat each ball with the pecans. Wrap loosely in wax paper, seal in a ziplock plastic bag, and refrigerate 2 hours (and up to 3 days) or until serving. Serve with the crackers.

———◆———

Lemon-Shallot Green Beans

Green beans are often on Southern funeral menus in the form of heavy casseroles. This simpler preparation brightens the flavors on the table and is a lot faster to make. Using a small amount of water to steam the beans saves the trouble of boiling and draining. To make ahead, cook the beans the day before and finish off in the skillet a few minutes in advance. If using lemon zest as garnish, take it off the lemon before you juice it.

serves 8

2 pounds fresh haricots verts (tiny French green beans), trimmed, or regular green beans, cut in half lengthwise

⅔ cup water

3 tablespoons olive oil

4 garlic cloves, minced

4 shallots, sliced

¼ cup chopped fresh basil

¼ cup fresh lemon juice

1 teaspoon table salt

¼ teaspoon freshly ground black pepper

Garnishes: strips of lemon zest, fresh basil leaves

1. Combine beans and water in a Dutch oven. Bring to a boil over high heat; cover. Cook 6 minutes. Uncover and cook until all of the water is evaporated, about 3 more minutes.

2. Heat olive oil in a large skillet over medium heat. Cook the garlic and shallots in hot oil for 2 minutes or until just golden brown; remove from the heat. Stir in the basil, lemon juice, salt, and pepper. Add the green beans, and toss to coat. Garnish, if desired.

———◆———

Buttermilk Yeast Rolls

Homemade yeast rolls are comforting for any occasion, but especially so during a time filled with grief. The combination of slightly sweet, dense dough with butter is just good for the soul. These rolls will freeze for up to a month ahead, so they can be ready anytime. Wrap the cooled rolls in foil, place in a ziplock plastic freezer bag, and freeze. Just reheat wrapped rolls in a 350°F oven for about 25 minutes.

makes 2 dozen

1 (¼-ounce) envelope active dry yeast

¼ cup warm water (105°F to 115°F)

2 tablespoons plus 1 teaspoon granulated sugar, divided

2 tablespoons unsalted butter, softened

1 teaspoon table salt

1 large egg

¾ cup whole buttermilk

½ cup milk

4 cups all-purpose flour

2 tablespoons melted unsalted butter

Garnish: flaky sea salt

1. Stir together the yeast, water, and 1 teaspoon sugar in a 2-cup glass measuring cup; let stand 5 minutes.

2. Beat remaining 2 tablespoons sugar, softened butter, and salt in the bowl of an electric stand mixer at medium speed until creamy. Add the egg, buttermilk, milk, and yeast mixture, beating until blended. Gradually add the flour, beating at low speed until smooth. Turn the dough out onto a well-floured surface, and knead until smooth and slightly elastic, about 2 to 3 minutes. Place in a well-greased bowl, turning to grease top.

3. Cover and let rise in a warm place (80°F to 85°F), free from drafts, 1 hour or until doubled in size.

4. Preheat the oven to 400°F. Punch the dough down. Turn the dough out onto a floured surface. Divide the dough into 24 pieces; shape into balls. Place in 2 greased 9-inch cake pans. Cover and let rise in a warm place (80°F to 85°F), free from drafts, 20 minutes. Some ovens have "proof" settings that will heat just slightly for rising dough. Another warm spot can often be found on top of the refrigerator.

5. Bake in the preheated oven for 15 minutes or until golden. Brush the tops with the melted butter, sprinkle with sea salt, if desired, and serve immediately.

Squash Casserole

If you haven't had the South's most comforting of casseroles, now is your time. Squash casseroles can be dressed up with anything from saltines to French fried onions to homemade breadcrumbs. My go-to recipe is the version from my childhood: a cheesy Southern classic that's covered in Ritz crackers. It would be sinful to skip the crackers and butter on top. Assemble the casserole in advance and refrigerate up to 12 hours, then let it stand at room temperature for 30 minutes before baking. Add the crackers just before going into the oven.

serves 8

3 pounds yellow squash, sliced into
　½-inch-thick slices

1 sweet onion, chopped (about 1 cup)

2 tablespoons olive oil

1½ teaspoons table salt, divided

½ teaspoon freshly ground black pepper

4 ounces shredded extra-sharp Cheddar
　cheese (1 cup)

2 large eggs, lightly beaten

¼ cup mayonnaise

20 round buttery crackers, such as
　Ritz, crushed (about ¾ cup)

2 tablespoons unsalted butter, melted

1. Preheat the oven to 400°F. Arrange the squash and onion on a rimmed baking sheet. The vegetables will not be in a single layer. Toss with olive oil and sprinkle with ½ teaspoon salt and pepper. Cook for 35 minutes, or until squash is tender when pricked with a fork. The squash will not be browned. Set aside and allow to cool slightly.

2. Lower oven temperature to 350°F. Combine cheese, egg, mayonnaise, and remaining 1 teaspoon salt in a large mixing bowl. Use a slotted spoon to transfer squash and onions from the baking sheet into the mixing bowl, discarding any liquid left on the baking sheet. Gently stir to combine. Spoon the mixture into a lightly greased 11- x 7-inch baking dish.

3. Stir together crushed crackers and melted butter; sprinkle evenly over the top of casserole. Bake at 350°F for 30 to 35 minutes or until bubbly and golden brown.

Roasted Beef Tenderloin

Having a funeral reception without a beef tenderloin is close to having one without a death. I have friends that keep one in the freezer at all times just in case an emergency funeral need arises. Seriously. I like to serve mine with a choice of sauces but this impressive cut can certainly stand on its own as well. Little sandwiches made with the tender beef are also a hit. Beef tenderloin is one of the few meats that's nearly as good at room temperature as it is warm. It's a make-ahead favorite so roast it off the day before or the morning of and serve at room temperature. The sauces can both be made a few days in advance.

serves 8 to 10

¼ cup whole black peppercorns

3 tablespoons kosher salt

1 (4½-pound) beef tenderloin, trimmed and tied

5 tablespoons extra-virgin olive oil, divided

Creamy Horseradish Sauce

Vidalia Onion Chimichurri

1. Preheat the oven to 350°F.

2. Use a coffee grinder or a mortar and pestle to coarsely grind peppercorns. Combine the peppercorns and the salt. Rub the tenderloin with 2 tablespoons of the olive oil until coated. Rub the pepper mixture over the tenderloin until generously coated. (You will think you have too much salt and pepper on the meat, but you don't.)

3. Using a 14-inch skillet or a stove-top-proof roasting pan or griddle, heat the remaining 3 tablespoons of olive oil over medium-high. Add the tenderloin, and cook on each side until deeply browned, about 5 minutes per side.

4. Place the tenderloin on a rimmed baking sheet, and bake in the preheated oven until a meat thermometer reaches 130°F to 140°F degrees (rare to medium-rare), about 30 to 40 minutes. Allow the meat to stand 20 minutes before slicing. Serve with the Creamy Horseradish Sauce and Vidalia Onion Chimichurri.

Creamy Horseradish Sauce

1 cup mayonnaise

¼ cup whipping cream

1 tablespoon Dijon mustard

¼ cup prepared horseradish, or more, if desired

Salt and freshly ground black pepper to taste

Whisk together the mayonnaise, whipping cream, mustard, and horseradish. Add more horseradish, if desired. Add the salt and pepper to taste. Cover and chill up to 4 days or until ready to serve. This makes 2 cups.

Vidalia Onion Chimichurri

⅔ cup olive oil

½ cup red wine vinegar

¾ cup diced sweet onion

⅔ cup chopped fresh flat-leaf parsley

1 teaspoon kosher salt

Whisk together all the ingredients. Cover and chill up to 2 days. Allow it to come to room temperature before serving. This makes 2 cups.

Our Supervisor General
. . . .

When each of my grandmothers passed away, our neighbor Becky Rawlins, a hostess with etiquette that extends beyond the levels most of us will ever reach, was at our house within an hour. She ensured our house was ready while my parents handled all the awful necessary details with the funeral home. Becky made sure our dining room was ready with flowers in the center of the table and double-checked all silver and china for serving. Visitors toting warm dishes and tall cakes were not far behind but a notebook was already waiting to write down condolences so thank-you notes could be written later. Thanks to Becky taking charge of our family's major life and death events, my dad nicknamed her our "Supervisor General."

Just Chess Pie

Chess pie is a Southern icon of desserts that's been around for generations. Most of its ingredients are kitchen staples, and the richness is hard to match in other pies. It's super sweet, so small slices are perfect. The custard filling needs to cool completely before slicing the pie, so make the pie the day before. If you have a tiny bit of filling left over, bake it for a few minutes in a ramekin for a cook's treat.

serves 8

1 purchased piecrust (or homemade)

2 cups granulated sugar

1 tablespoon all-purpose flour

1½ tablespoons plain yellow cornmeal

⅓ cup milk

¼ cup unsalted butter, melted

1 tablespoon white vinegar

½ teaspoon vanilla extract

4 large eggs, lightly beaten

Whipped cream (optional)

1. Preheat the oven to 425°F. Fit the pastry into a 9-inch pie plate according to the package directions; fold edges under, and crimp. Line the piecrust with aluminum foil, and fill with pie weights or dried beans.

2. Bake in the preheated oven for 7 minutes. Remove the weights and foil, and bake for 4 more minutes. The crust edges will look only slightly browned and the bottom will not look done. Gently press down any bubbles in the crust with the back of a spoon and set crust aside. Reduce the oven temperature to 350°F.

3. Whisk together the sugar, flour, and cornmeal until blended in a medium mixing bowl.

4. Whisk together milk and next 3 ingredients in a small bowl. Whisk milk mixture into sugar mixture. Add the eggs, whisking until no yellow from the yolks can be seen. Pour the mixture into the prepared piecrust.

5. Bake in the preheated oven for 50 to 55 minutes or until golden, shielding edges of crust with aluminum foil to prevent excessive browning, if necessary. Cool completely on a wire rack. Serve with the whipped cream, if desired.

Tailgate at Home

We live 2.5 miles from Sanford Stadium. If you know SEC football, you know what that means. We can wake up on game days in the fall and the University of Georgia's Redcoat Marching Band is warming up in the distance. There's nothing like living in a college town. Electricity fills the air during home games that is passionate and contagious. Tailgating takes place on every inch of campus to a point that I can't imagine what the grass looked like the day before. On Saturdays that take the Dawgs out of town, it's time to set up tailgate at our house and cheer them on from afar.

Early Afternoon

Tarragon Deviled Eggs

Fancy Hot Dogs

Chicken Tomatillo Chili

Slow-Cooker Queso

Grilled Succotash Salad

Coca-Cola Cake

Timeline

1 to 2 Days Earlier
- Set out all serving dishes with labels, plates, utensils, glasses, and napkins.
- Make salad, cover, and store in the refrigerator.
- Chill wine, beer, and mixers to be served.
- Set up bar with glasses, ice bucket, and other hardware needed.

1 Day Earlier
- Cut a slit in hot dogs, and store in a ziplock plastic bag in the refrigerator.
- Make sauce for hot dogs, and refrigerate.
- Make chili, cover, and store in the refrigerator.
- Slice fruit for the bar.

Night Before
- Boil eggs and make the filling. Store the filling in a ziplock plastic bag in the refrigerator, squeezing out as much air as possible. Store egg whites on a paper towel-lined plate, covered in plastic wrap.
- Make Coca-Cola Cake and frost. Store at room temperature in baking pan, covered with foil (carefully as to not smudge the icing).

4 Hours Earlier
- Zip around for last-minute cleaning in the house.

3 Hours Earlier
- Run the dishwasher for the last time before guests arrive.

2 Hours Earlier
- Start queso dip in the slow cooker.

1 Hour Earlier
- Unload any clean dishes from dishwasher.

45 Minutes Earlier
- Preheat oven to 350°F for baking hot dogs.
- Arrange hot dogs in baking dish, and cover with sauce.
- Dab egg whites with paper towel, if needed. Pipe filling into egg whites.

30 Minutes Earlier
- Bake hot dogs for 20 minutes.
- Simmer chili on the stove-top to reheat.

15 Minutes Earlier
- Take out the trash.

Tarragon Deviled Eggs

Deviled eggs are a mainstay for any hostess. I've never had a party where one was left over. Make sure to buy your eggs a few days in advance. Older eggs peel easier and cause less cursing in the kitchen. I make deviled eggs ahead by keeping the filling in a large ziplock plastic bag, with the air squeezed out as much as possible. Just squeeze the filling into the whites before a party.

makes 24 deviled eggs

12 large eggs	1 teaspoon Dijon mustard
⅓ cup mayonnaise	⅛ teaspoon table salt
3 tablespoons dill pickle juice	⅛ teaspoon freshly ground black pepper
1 tablespoon chopped fresh tarragon	Garnish: chopped fresh tarragon

1. Place the eggs in a single layer in a saucepan. Add water to cover by 1 inch. Bring to a boil; cover, remove from the heat, and let stand 10 minutes. Drain. Submerge the eggs in cold water. Tap each egg firmly on the counter until cracks form all over the shell. Peel under cold running water.

2. Slice the eggs in half lengthwise; carefully remove the yolks, keeping the egg white halves intact.

3. Using the fine holes on a box grater, grate the yolks into a bowl. (Grating the yolks makes the creamiest filling.) Stir in the mayonnaise and next 5 ingredients. Spoon or pipe the filling into the whites. Garnish, if desired.

———◆———

Fancy Hot Dogs

One of the best hostesses I've ever known was our next-door neighbor while I was growing up. Becky Rawlins seemed to be able to host a handful of friends or a few dozen guests without batting an eye. She did flowers, cooked like a pro, and was even known to keep her house scented to perfection thanks to spritzing rooms with her favorite perfume. She made a recipe very similar to this one countless times. When she hosted our youth group at church for Sunday suppers, these were always on the menu. Make the sauce ahead and even slit the hot dogs in advance. Assemble and bake before serving.

serves 8 to 10

1 tablespoon unsalted butter	1 teaspoon freshly ground black pepper
1 sweet onion, diced (about 1 cup)	½ teaspoon hot sauce
½ cup ketchup	2 (12-ounce) packs bun-length beef
⅓ cup apple cider vinegar	franks (I use Hebrew National)
3 tablespoons light brown sugar	14 hot dogs buns
1 tablespoon Worcestershire sauce	
2 teaspoons paprika	
2 teaspoons yellow mustard	

1. Preheat the oven to 350°F. Melt the butter in a large ovenproof skillet over medium. Add the onions, and cook until soft, about 4 to 6 minutes. Add the ketchup and next 7 ingredients. Stir to combine. Remove from the heat.

2. Cut a small slit down the length of each hot dog (about 4 inches long). Place the hot dogs, slit sides up, in the skillet and spoon the sauce over to coat all the hot dogs. Bake at 350°F for 20 minutes, basting three times.

3. Serve the hot dogs in the buns with the extra sauce spooned over.

———◆———

Chicken Tomatillo Chili

One of the very few foods I don't like is kidney beans. It's my own fault that for years I have been left out of the all the chili camaraderie at tailgates and parties. White chili made with chicken and white beans has always been my solution. I've just recently started adding tomatillos. They add a nice tartness and brighten up the entire batch. Make this up to two days in advance and just reheat on the stove-top to serve.

serves 8

3 tablespoons olive oil	4 cups chicken broth
1 onion, diced (about 1 ⅓ cups)	2 (15-ounce) cans navy beans, drained
1 jalapeño, seeded and diced (about	and rinsed
2 tablespoons)	¾ teaspoon table salt
1 garlic clove, minced (about 1 teaspoon)	2 pounds boneless, skinless chicken
1 pound tomatillos	breasts, cut into ¾-inch pieces
2 teaspoons dried oregano	Garnishes: fresh cilantro, sour cream,
1 teaspoon ground cumin	avocado, shredded Monterey Jack cheese

1. Heat the olive oil in a large Dutch oven over medium. Add the onion, jalapeño, and garlic, and sauté for 5 minutes or until just starting to brown.

2. Peel the papery husks from the tomatillos. Rinse the tomatillos in warm water to remove the sticky residue that the husks leave behind. Chop the tomatillos, and add to the onion mixture. Add the oregano and cumin, stirring to combine. Cook for 6 to 7 minutes to soften the tomatillos.

3. Add the broth, beans, and salt; bring to a boil over medium-high. Reduce the heat to medium, and simmer 20 minutes. Add the chicken and cook until done, about 5 minutes. Serve with the cilantro, sour cream, avocado, and cheese, if desired. This yields 10 ½ cups of chili.

Slow-Cooker Queso

I could eat my weight in cheese dip each and every time we go to a Mexican restaurant. It's a problem. So, of course I like to make a huge batch at home so all my guests can do the same thing. The slow cooker saves all the stirring and keeps the temperature low enough so that the cheese doesn't burn. Buy the white American cheese fresh sliced from the deli counter at your grocery store. They'll look at you like you're crazy when you order 1½ pounds, but it's worth the stares.

serves 8 to 10

2 tablespoons olive oil

1 onion, diced (1 cup)

2 garlic cloves, minced

1 (10-ounce) can diced tomatoes and green chiles, drained

1 (4-ounce) can diced jalapeños, undrained

1½ pounds white American cheese slices, torn into pieces

¾ cup whole milk

Tortilla chips

Garnish: sliced scallions

1. Heat the olive oil in a skillet over medium. Add the onion and garlic, and cook for 4 minutes or until just starting to soften.

2. Transfer the mixture to a 6-quart slow cooker. Add the tomatoes and chiles, jalapeños, cheese, and milk. Stir, keeping in mind the torn cheese will look like a mess, and cover with the slow cooker lid. Cook on HIGH for 10 minutes. Lower the heat to LOW, and cook for 1 hour and 40 minutes. (Feel free to lift the lid and stir while it's cooking if it looks like it needs it.)

3. Reduce the heat to WARM to keep the dip ready for guests. Serve with the tortilla chips. Garnish if desired.

A Tailgate Refresher

Football kicks off in the Deep South when the weather is still offering the full force of blazing heat and thick humidity. Buy some inexpensive white washcloths in time for the tailgate. Soak them in water with a few drops of essential oils (lavender and lime are my favorites). Chill the towels in the refrigerator overnight. Small coolers can be placed around with the chilled towels for guests to refresh. Fans will no doubt appreciate the quick and calming cooldown.

Grilled Succotash Salad

Taking succotash to the grill makes for a salad that bursts with color as much as flavor. The dressing is lemony-light and is reminiscent of the finest of homemade Southern slaws. Make it up to three days in advance and keep chilled in the refrigerator. Just stir in the fresh basil right before serving.

serves 8

1 pound fresh or frozen butter beans

4 ears fresh corn, husks removed

1 large red onion, cut into thick slices

1 large red bell pepper, cut into thick rings

3 tablespoons olive oil

1 teaspoon table salt, divided

1 teaspoon freshly ground black pepper, divided

½ cup mayonnaise

3 tablespoons white wine vinegar

1 tablespoon Dijon mustard

1 tablespoon granulated sugar

Zest of 1 lemon

1 cup halved grape tomatoes

¼ cup chopped fresh basil

1. Cook the fresh butter beans in salted boiling water for 30 minutes or until tender. Drain. If using frozen, cook according to package directions; drain. Cool completely, about 20 minutes.

2. Meanwhile, preheat the grill to medium heat (350°F). Brush corn, onion, and pepper with olive oil. Sprinkle with ½ teaspoon salt and ½ teaspoon black pepper. Grill the corn, covered with the grill lid, 15 minutes or until just beginning to char, turning every 4 to 5 minutes. Grill the onion and bell pepper, covered with the grill lid, 5 minutes on each side or until tender. Cool all the vegetables completely, about 20 minutes.

3. Cut the kernels from the cobs. Discard the cobs. Chop the onion and bell pepper into ½-inch pieces.

4. Stir together the mayonnaise and next 4 ingredients in a large mixing bowl. Gently fold in the tomatoes, corn kernels, chopped onion and pepper, and remaining ½ teaspoon salt and ½ teaspoon pepper. Cover and chill at least 2 hours before serving. Store in the refrigerator for up to 3 days. Add basil just before serving.

Coca-Cola Cake

Southerners tend to cook with the soda that calls Georgia home almost as much as we drink it. It gives a perfect sweetness to balance the tang of buttermilk and an airiness that only comes from carbonation. The frosting is best made while this easy sheet cake is baking so it can be poured right over the warm cake. You can garnish the cake with just about anything from marshmallows to pecans to chocolate chips to pretzels. There's really no wrong choice. Make ahead or send a piece home with tailgaters. The frosted cake can be stored at room temperature for one day.

serves 12

1 cup Coca-Cola soft drink	2 cups all-purpose flour
½ cup whole buttermilk	3 tablespoons unsweetened cocoa powder
¾ cup unsalted butter, softened	1 teaspoon baking soda
1½ cups granulated sugar	1 cup miniature marshmallows
2 large eggs, lightly beaten	Coca-Cola Frosting
2 teaspoons vanilla extract	Garnish: ¾ cup chopped toasted pecans

1. Preheat the oven to 350°F. Combine the Coca-Cola and buttermilk; set aside.

2. Beat the butter with an electric mixer at low speed until creamy. Gradually add the sugar and beat until blended. Add the eggs and vanilla and beat at low speed until blended.

3. Combine the flour, cocoa, and baking soda. Add to the butter mixture alternately with the cola mixture, beginning and ending with the flour mixture. Beat at low speed just until blended.

4. Stir in the marshmallows. Pour the batter into a greased and floured 13 x 9-inch pan. Bake in the preheated oven for 30 minutes. The marshmallows will have risen to the top of the cake. Remove from the oven; cool on a wire rack 10 minutes. Pour the Coca-Cola Frosting over the warm cake while still in the pan; garnish, if desired.

Coca-Cola Frosting

½ cup unsalted butter	1 (16-ounce) package powdered sugar
¼ cup Coca-Cola soft drink	(3½ cups)
3 tablespoons unsweetened cocoa powder	1 tablespoon vanilla extract

Combine the butter and Coca-Cola in a large saucepan over medium heat, stirring until the butter melts. Remove from the heat; whisk in the cocoa, sugar, and vanilla. Pour warm icing over the cake. Makes 2¼ cups.

Drinks on the Porch

I t's true we have really good times on porches in the South. From shelling peas and shucking corn to clinking glasses and listening to a little gossip. It's the place to be. Having friends over for a homemade happy hour is always appropriate. Gathering on the porch is more casual than an inside event and will probably last only until the sun goes down. If you don't have a good porch, make a friend who does. You can bring the drinks and she can provide the outdoors.

5 p.m.

Blue Cheese Two-Pepper Wafers

Herb and Orange Marinated Olives

Sinful Butter Saltines

Ginger Wine Spritzer

Peach Mojitos

Tart Cherry Limeade

Timeline

3 Days Earlier
- Make olives. Store in refrigerator in a ziplock plastic bag.
- Cut candied ginger into strips for garnish on spritzers. Store at room temperature.

2 Days Earlier
- Set out all serving dishes with labels, plates, utensils, pitchers, and glasses. Set out napkins.
- Chill club soda and Riesling wine.
- Chill any additional wine, beer, and mixers to be served.
- Set up bar with glasses, ice bucket, and other hardware needed.
- Turn olive bag over to marinate evenly.

1 Day Earlier
- Make dough for cheese straws and chill.
- Make saltines. Store at room temperature.

- Turn olive bag over to marinate evenly.
- Slice fruit for the bar.

Night Before
- Process peach mixture in a blender or food processor for mojitos. Cover and refrigerate.
- Blend whole lime mixture. Cover and refrigerate.
- Slice lime for garnish on limeade. Store in a ziplock plastic bag in the refrigerator.

4 Hours, 30 Minutes Earlier
- Preheat oven to 375°F for baking cheese straws.

4 Hours Earlier
- Zip around for last-minute cleaning in the house.
- Bake cheese straws for 20 minutes. Cool and store at room temperature.

3 Hours Earlier
- Run the dishwasher for the last time before guests arrive.

2 Hours Earlier
- Combine Riesling wine and bitters for spritzer.

1 Hour Earlier
- Unload any clean dishes from dishwasher.

45 Minutes Earlier
- Add cherry juice to limeade.
- Muddle mint and stir together mojitos.

30 Minutes Earlier
- Take out the trash.

15 Minutes Earlier
- Add club soda to spritzers.

Herb and Orange Marinated Olives

A little something salty always adds to the cocktail hour and nearly everyone loves olives. I keep these in my fridge just about all the time so they are ready when an unexpected guest drops in. Look for good quality olives on the pickle aisle or choose your own blend at the olive bar. You can't go wrong. They need to be made days in advance, making them the perfect appetizer for parties of any kind.

makes 5 ½ cups

2 (6-ounce) jars pitted green Greek olives, drained (3 cups)

2 (6-ounce) jars pitted kalamata olives, drained (2 cups)

1 lemon

1 orange

¾ cup olive oil

4 garlic cloves, thinly sliced

2 tablespoons fresh thyme leaves

2 tablespoons chopped fresh rosemary

1 teaspoon crushed red pepper

1. Combine the olives in a large ziplock plastic bag.

2. Zest both the lemon and orange with a strip zester to make little ribbons of peel. After zesting, juice both the lemon and orange. You will have about 2 tablespoons lemon juice and ¼ cup orange juice. Add the zest, juice, and the next 5 ingredients to the olives. Seal the bag, and shake to mix.

3. Refrigerate for 3 days, turning the bag once a day. Allow the olives to come to room temperature to liquefy the olive oil before serving with a slotted spoon.

Sinful Butter Saltines

Saltines baked with butter are well known around dining rooms in a couple of Atlanta's most prestigious country clubs. Offered as a beginning to a meal, like bread often is, they have been a mainstay for years. The chefs in the clubhouses use clarified butter, but for making at home, I use ghee. Common in Indian cooking, ghee is clarified butter that has been cooked to have a slightly nutty flavor. Look for it in the international section of the grocery store (not the refrigerator case). These buttery goodies can be made one day ahead and kept at room temperature in an airtight container.

serves 8

1¼ cups ghee

2 sleeves saltine crackers (I find Nabisco Premium get the crispiest)

1. Preheat the oven to 400°F. Melt the ghee in a saucepan over low. Transfer to a bowl, and add the saltines. Toss gently to coat each cracker with the butter.

2. Arrange the crackers in a single layer on a rimmed baking sheet. Bake at 400°F for 7 to 8 minutes (No need to turn the saltines. The crackers will be golden brown. This makes 68 crackers.) Serve warm or at room temperature.

Two-Pepper Blue Cheese Wafers

Cocktail hour always needs a little bite of something cheesy and crispy. Gorgonzola, black pepper, and a pinch of cayenne pepper make for a fun twist on a classic Southern cheese straw. Make the dough the day before and bake them the morning of the party.

makes about 32

½ cup unsalted butter, softened

7 ounces Gorgonzola blue cheese, crumbled, at room temperature

½ teaspoon freshly ground black pepper, plus more for sprinkling

⅛ teaspoon cayenne pepper

1½ cups all-purpose flour

1. Combine all ingredients in the bowl of a food processor fitted with the metal blade. Process until mixture forms a dough.

2. Shape the dough into a log about 12 inches long. Wrap in plastic wrap; chill 3 to 24 hours.

3. Preheat the oven to 375°F. Cut the log into ⅓-inch-thick slices. Place 2 inches apart on parchment paper-lined baking sheets. Sprinkle with additional black pepper. Bake, in batches, 18 to 20 minutes or until golden brown. Cool on pans for 5 minutes. Transfer to a wire rack, and cool completely, about 20 minutes.

———◆———

Tart Cherry Limeade

Nonalcoholic drinks should be just as interesting as those with a little libation. Taking entire limes and zipping them around in a blender is fun and a great conversation starter! Look for tart cherry juice in the juice section with unsweetened and 100% juices.

serves 8

2 limes, ends removed, quartered and seeded

1¼ cups granulated sugar

4 cups water

2½ cups pure tart cherry juice (100% juice, no added sweeteners, unconcentrated)

Ice

1½ cups (12 ounces) club soda

Garnish: lime slices

1. Process the limes, sugar, and 4 cups water in a blender until frothy and the sound of limes hitting the blades has stopped being so loud, 1 to 2 minutes. Pour through a fine-mesh strainer into a pitcher. Discard the solids. Chill until ready to serve. Add the cherry juice, and stir to combine.

2. Pour over glasses filled with the ice, and top with a splash of club soda and a lime slice.

Ginger Wine Spritzer

Wine spritzers were crazy popular in the 1980s, and they've made a pleasant comeback. It's a great way to serve a cocktail that's a little less potent. This refreshing, not-too-sweet sipper can be made ahead by stirring the wine and bitters together in advance. Add the club soda just before serving.

serves 8

2 (750-milliliter) bottles dry Riesling wine

2 cups club soda

½ ounce (1 tablespoon) ginger bitters

Ice

Combine the wine, club soda, and bitters in a pitcher. Stir to combine. This makes about 9 cups. Serve over the ice in a wineglass.

Peach Mojitos

I remember the exact moment I first tasted a mojito. I learned the delights of Cuban rum on a trip to France almost 20 years ago. One sip in a seaside café in Saint-Jean-Cap-Ferrat was all it took. My dear friend Virginia Willis makes a version with peaches that inspires me to do more than sip on my Georgia front porch. Process the peaches in advance and assemble in a pitcher right before guests arrive.

If you need to use frozen peeled peaches, the mojitos will be lighter in color. The rich golden pinks in peach skin darken the drink to a beautiful rose-like blush.

serves 8

1½ pounds (3 medium) ripe peaches, unpeeled, pitted and chopped, or 2 cups sliced frozen peaches, thawed

⅔ cup granulated sugar

½ cup fresh lime juice (from about 4 limes)

½ cup firmly packed fresh mint leaves

4 cups club soda, chilled

2 cups white rum (Havana Club is my favorite duty-free souvenir from any trip abroad)

Garnishes: fresh mint sprigs, peach wedges

1. Process the first 3 ingredients in a blender or food processor until smooth. This yields about 2½ cups.

2. Muddle the mint leaves against the bottom and sides of a glass pitcher to release the flavors. The leaves should be bruised and torn. Add the club soda, rum, and peach mixture; stir to combine. Serve immediately over ice. Garnish, if desired.

Sunset Summer Barbecue

Barbecues are one of the easiest, most relaxed ways to host a party. Warm weather and hot grills keep guests lingering outside so your timeline can be much less rigid. I find it even more fun for everyone if the host is grilling while the guests are enjoying the great outdoors. Let them congregate and relax while the smoke billows into the summer sky.

6 p.m.

Coca-Cola BBQ and Bacon Shrimp
Cheeseburgers with Fig and Red Onion Jam
Orange and Cilantro Slaw
Make-Ahead Luxury Cheese Grits
Easy Peach and Oats Cobbler
Vanilla Bean Ice Cream

Timeline

5 Days Earlier
- Make barbecue sauce. Cover and chill.

1 to 2 Days Earlier
- Set out all serving dishes with labels, plates, utensils, and glasses. Set out napkins.
- Make ice cream custard mixture. Cover and chill.
- Make grits, cover, and chill.
- Chill wine, beer, and mixers to be served.
- Set up bar with glasses, ice bucket, and other hardware needed.

1 Day Earlier
- Make onion jam for burgers. Refrigerate.
- Freeze ice cream in an electric ice cream maker. Store in freezer until serving.
- Make dressing for slaw. Chill until serving.
- Slice fruit for the bar.

Night Before
- Form burger patties. Stack, with foil or wax paper between patties, and seal in a large ziplock plastic bag. Refrigerate.
- Peel and wrap shrimp with bacon.

4 Hours Earlier
- Zip around for last-minute cleaning in the house.
- Peel, pit, and slice peaches for cobbler. Store in a ziplock bag until assembly.

3 Hours, 30 Minutes Earlier
- Slice vegetables for slaw. Keep covered with a damp paper towel in the fridge.

3 Hours Earlier
- Run the dishwasher for the last time before guests arrive.

1 Hour, 30 Minutes Earlier
- Preheat oven to 325°F for baking grits.

- Set grits out on counter to warm slightly.

1 Hour Earlier
- Unload any clean dishes from dishwasher.
- Bake grits for 50 minutes to 1 hour. Then raise oven temperature to 375°F for cobbler.

30 Minutes Earlier
- Take out the trash.
- Reheat onion jam on the stove-top. Keep warm.

25 Minutes Earlier
- Preheat the grill to 350°F to 400°F.
- Assemble cobbler and bake.

15 Minutes Earlier
- Assemble slaw.
- Grill shrimp.

Make-Ahead Luxury Cheese Grits

Make-ahead grits usually turn out far from how you had hoped. With this method of lots of cheese, butter, and eggs, you won't be disappointed. The rich ingredients save the cook from stirring during the party.

serves 8

1½ cups uncooked stone-ground grits

6 cups chicken broth

¼ cup unsalted butter

1 (8-ounce) log goat cheese (about 2 cups crumbled)

⅓ cup grated Parmigiano-Reggiano cheese

3 large eggs, beaten

1. Bring the grits and chicken broth to a simmer in a large Dutch oven. Simmer for 1 hour, stirring very often. Make sure you scrape down the sides and the bottom of the pot to keep them from sticking. (I like to use a fish spatula for my grits.) Carefully transfer the hot grits to a large bowl.

2. Fold in the butter and cheeses, and stir until melted. Add the eggs, and stir until completely incorporated. Pour into a greased 13- x 9-inch casserole dish. Cover and chill overnight.

3. Preheat the oven to 325°F. Remove the grits from the refrigerator, and let stand at room temperature for 30 minutes. Bake, uncovered, for 50 minutes to 1 hour or until light golden and slightly puffed.

Coca-Cola BBQ and Bacon Shrimp

Appetizers on the grill are always fun when everyone can congregate outside with a cold drink. The most time-consuming part of this recipe is peeling the shrimp and wrapping them with bacon. Go ahead and knock that out in advance and keep covered in the fridge until it's time to heat up the grill. If you have a sweet fishmonger, ask for peeled, tail-on shrimp. It's worth a try. The barbecue sauce can be made five days in advance and kept in the fridge until needed.

serves 8

1 cup ketchup

¾ cup Coca-Cola

¼ cup Worcestershire sauce

Zest and juice of 1 lemon

1 tablespoon light brown sugar

¼ teaspoon garlic powder

⅛ teaspoon cayenne pepper

¼ teaspoon onion powder

¼ teaspoon freshly ground black pepper

1 (12-ounce) package bacon (8 slices), (not thick-sliced)

1 pound (26 to 30) extra-large raw shrimp, peeled (with tails on)

Wooden picks

1. Combine the ketchup and next 8 ingredients in a medium saucepan over low. Bring to a simmer, stirring occasionally. Cook over low for 10 minutes. Set aside ½ cup of the sauce for basting; chill the remaining sauce until serving.
2. Cut each slice of bacon into 4 smaller slices. Wrap a small slice around each shrimp, and secure with a wooden pick. Brush about ⅔ cup of sauce on the shrimp.
3. Preheat a gas grill to medium (400°F to 450°F). Place the shrimp on oiled grates; grill for 8 to 10 minutes, brushing once with ½ cup of the reserved sauce. Serve with the remaining sauce.

———◆———

Orange and Cilantro Slaw

Thank goodness slaw has come a long way from the bags and bottles in the produce section. I like to slice all my vegetables and keep them in the fridge, covered with a damp paper towel. I make the dressing ahead and then add it all together right before the doorbell rings.

serves 8

⅓ cup mayonnaise

¼ cup white wine vinegar

3 tablespoons whole-grain mustard

Zest of 1 orange (about 1 tablespoon)

¼ cup fresh orange juice

¾ teaspoon table salt

¼ teaspoon freshly ground black pepper

6 cups thinly sliced savoy or napa cabbage

½ red onion, sliced into thin strips (about 4 ounces)

3 carrots, cut into strips using a peeler

1 cup chopped cilantro

Whisk together the mayonnaise and next 6 ingredients in a large bowl. Add the cabbage and the next 3 ingredients, and toss to coat with the dressing. Serve immediately.

Cheeseburgers with Fig and Red Onion Jam

I have never turned down a cheeseburger in my life. The juiciest burgers are gently formed, even so much so that you can still see the squiggly pattern of the meat when it was ground. Forming your burgers the day before also saves time when firing up the grill. Make the Fig and Red Onion Jam in advance and just reheat before serving. The sweet tangy relish-like flavor is dreamy on just about anything grilled from burgers to barbecue to hot dogs. Try the jam as an extra goodie on a platter of cheese and charcuterie (page 222).

serves 8

3 pounds ground chuck

1 teaspoon table salt

1 teaspoon freshly ground black pepper

8 (½-ounce) slices white Cheddar cheese

8 brioche hamburger buns, toasted

Fig and Red Onion Jam

1. Coat the cold grate of the grill with cooking spray, and place on the grill. Preheat the grill to medium (about 350°F). Gently shape the ground chuck into 8 patties, each about ½ inch thick. Sprinkle one side of burgers with salt and pepper.
2. Grill the patties, covered, 5 minutes on each side. Top with cheese; grill, covered, for 2 more minutes or until the beef is no longer pink in the center and the cheese is melted. Serve the burgers on the buns with a generous dollop of desired amount of Fig and Red Onion Jam.

Fig and Red Onion Jam

4 cups thinly sliced red onions (from about 2 medium)

3 tablespoons unsalted butter

¼ cup firmly packed light brown sugar

½ cup red wine vinegar

⅓ cup fig preserves

Sauté the onions in butter in a Dutch oven over medium-low 10 minutes or until limber and barely beginning to brown. Reduce the heat to low; stir in the sugar, vinegar, and preserves. Cook 12 minutes or until onions are deep golden brown and starting to look a little syrupy. Set aside while cheeseburgers are grilling. Jam can be made ahead and chilled for up to 3 days. Warm before serving. Makes 1½ cups.

Easy Peach and Oats Cobbler

I learned the art of easy cobblers (among other things) from Nathalie Dupree. It's my go-to dessert for summer parties.

serves 8

½ cup unsalted butter

1 cup all-purpose soft-wheat flour (such as White Lily)

1¼ cups granulated sugar

¾ cup uncooked old-fashioned oats

1 tablespoon plus ½ teaspoon baking powder

½ teaspoon ground cinnamon

⅛ teaspoon table salt

1½ cups whole milk

1 teaspoon vanilla extract

4 cups peeled, pitted, and sliced peaches (1½ pounds frozen, thawed)

1. Preheat the oven to 375°F. In a 10-inch cast-iron skillet, melt the butter in the oven while it's preheating. Once the butter is melted, remove the skillet from the oven.

2. Whisk together the flour and next 5 ingredients in a bowl. Whisk in the milk and vanilla.

3. Pour the batter over the melted butter in the hot skillet. (The butter will sizzle slightly and rise over the sides of the batter.) Arrange the peaches evenly over the batter.

4. Bake at 375°F for 45 to 50 minutes or until deep golden brown and shimmery with tiny bubbles. Serve hot, warm, or at room temperature.

Vanilla Bean Ice Cream

You can make the entire recipe in advance and scoop out servings as you would any other ice cream. Another choice (and my favorite) is to have the custard ready to pour into the ice-cream maker and let the guests be filled with anticipation as the machine spins in the kitchen.

serves 8 (makes about 1 quart)

¾ cup granulated sugar

2 tablespoons cornstarch

⅛ teaspoon table salt

1½ cups milk

1½ cups half-and-half

2 large egg yolks

1 vanilla bean, split lengthwise

1. Whisk together the first 5 ingredients in a large heavy saucepan. Gradually whisk in the milk and half-and-half. Cook over medium heat, stirring constantly, 10 to 12 minutes or until the mixture thickens slightly. Do not simmer. Remove from the heat.

2. Whisk the egg yolks together until slightly thickened in a medium mixing bowl. Gradually whisk about 1 cup of the hot milk mixture into the yolks, then pour them into the remaining hot mixture, whisking constantly. Scrape seeds from vanilla bean into the hot mixture. Allow to cool 30 minutes, stirring occasionally.

3. Place plastic wrap directly on the surface of the custard (to prevent a film from forming), and chill 8 to 24 hours.

4. Pour the custard into the freezer container of a 1½-quart electric ice-cream maker, and freeze according to the manufacturer's instructions.

Supper Club with Friends

If you're not a member of a supper club, it's time to start one. Belonging to a supper club pretty much guarantees you won't lose touch with friends, even in the busiest of times. Make it a priority to be an active member of the club. Six to eight members make it manageable to host as well as small enough to be able to visit with everyone throughout the evening. Plan on meeting several times a year to keep the momentum going. A supper club with good food and fun members will thrive each time.

7 p.m.

Southern Cheese and
Charcuterie Platter
Chicken and Collards Pilau
Loaded Skillet Cornbread
Green Goddess Romaine Salad
Slow-Cooker Apple Crisp

Timeline

1 to 2 Days Earlier
- Set out all serving dishes with labels, plates, utensils, and glasses. Set out napkins.
- Make green goddess dressing. Cover and refrigerate.
- Chill wine, beer, and mixers to be served.
- Set up bar with glasses, ice bucket, and other hardware needed.

1 Day Earlier
- Combine flour, brown sugar, and butter mixture for crisp. Store in a ziplock plastic bag in refrigerator.
- Make cornbread. Cool completely, and store, covered, at room temperature.
- Slice fruit for the bar.

Night Before
- Dice and cube sausage and chicken for pilau, and refrigerate separately in ziplock plastic bags.
- Chop vegetables for pilau. Refrigerate.

4 Hours Earlier
- Zip around for last-minute cleaning in the house.

3 Hours Earlier
- Run the dishwasher for the last time before guests arrive.
- Begin to assemble crisp in slow cooker. Turn on HIGH for 3 hours.

1 Hour Earlier
- Unload any clean dishes from dishwasher.
- Cut romaine hearts into quarters for salad. Cover with a damp paper towel.

45 Minutes Earlier
- Arrange cheese on charcuterie platter to soften.

30 Minutes Earlier
- Take out the trash.
- Preheat oven to 400°F for reheating cornbread.

25 Minutes Earlier
- Add charcuterie to platter.

15 Minutes Earlier
- Reheat cornbread for about 10 minutes or until warm.

Southern Cheese and Charcuterie Platter

Putting together a successful charcuterie and cheese platter takes minimal effort with splendid results. The key is not stressing about exactly what you choose to showcase. No matter what I've ever served in a selection, I've never heard a complaint.

serving per person: 3 slices of meat and 2 ounces of cheese

For the charcuterie, I like to offer at least three different meats. My favorites are shaved country ham, peppery salami, and prosciutto. I also like pastrami and a really good pepperoni. Set out the charcuterie about 25 minutes in advance so it can warm slightly before serving. Set out a separate fork for each meat.

For the cheese, try offering a soft, a firm, a mild blue, and your favorite pimiento cheese. Each cheese will require its own knife. There's only one hard and fast rule: no cheese cubes under any circumstances. For the best temperature and softness, set out the cheeses on the counter about 45 minutes early to soften.

For accompaniments, try whole-grain mustard, pepper jelly, sorghum, toasted pecans, halved figs, and some bread and butter pickles. Crackers and bread are always welcome on my platters, but I prefer ones that aren't strongly flavored so the meat and cheese can really shine.

There's no need to buy a fancy wooden serving board for charcuterie and cheese at home. Any large platter, cutting board, or stone slab (as long as it's food-safe) will work wonderfully.

It would be impossible to name all the talented artisans making Southern charcuterie and cheeses. Here are just a few to get you started. Make sure to research what's closest to your area. The closer to home, the better.

Cheese
· · · ·

Blackberryfarmshop.com
Brazos Valley Cheese, Waco, Texas
CalyRoad Creamery, Sandy Springs, Georgia
Dayspring Dairy, Gallant, Alabama
Fromagerie Belle Chevre, Elkmont, Alabama
Sweet Grass Dairy, Thomasville, Georgia

Charcuterie
· · · · · · · ·

Blackberryfarmshop.com
Ted's Butcherblock, Charleston, South Carolina
Heywood's Provision Company, Marietta, Georgia
Pendulum Fine Meats, Norfolk, Virginia
Pine Street Market, Avondale Estates, Georgia
Edwardsvaham.com for 400-day aged Surryano ham
The Spotted Trotter Charcuterie, Atlanta, Georgia

Chicken and Collards Pilau

The combination of spicy sausage, salty bacon, comforting collards, chicken thighs, and rice is nearly impossible to beat. It's easy to make a day in advance and simply reheat before serving.

serves 6 to 8

4 ounces andouille sausage, diced

3 ounces thick-sliced bacon (2 slices), chopped

1½ pounds skinless, boneless chicken thighs, cubed

1¼ teaspoons table salt

½ teaspoon freshly ground black pepper

2 tablespoons olive oil

1 large leek, white and light green parts only, thinly sliced

1 cup chopped celery

1 cup chopped carrot

½ cup chopped sweet onion

3 garlic cloves, minced

3 cups chicken broth

¼ cup fresh lemon juice (from 1 large lemon)

4 cups firmly packed chopped fresh collard greens, about 1 pound before trimming

2 cups uncooked jasmine rice

Hot sauce and lemon wedges, for serving

1. Preheat the oven to 350°F. Cook the sausage and bacon in a Dutch oven over medium-high heat, stirring often, 10 to 12 minutes or until browned. Remove using a slotted spoon, reserving the drippings in the pan.

2. Sprinkle the chicken with salt and pepper. Add the oil to the hot drippings in the Dutch oven, and cook the chicken in the hot drippings over medium-high heat, stirring occasionally, 8 to 10 minutes or until done. Add the leek and next 4 ingredients. Cook, stirring often, 5 to 7 minutes or until the vegetables are tender. Stir in the broth and the next 3 ingredients. Add the sausage and bacon back to the pan.

3. Bring the mixture to a boil over medium-high heat. Remove from the heat; cover.

4. Transfer to the oven and bake the pilau for 20 to 25 minutes or until the liquid is absorbed, stirring halfway through.

5. Serve with hot sauce and a squeeze of lemon, if desired.

———◆———

Loaded Skillet Cornbread

I've never met a person who didn't like cornbread. And if you know of someone, this will convert them on the spot. It's heavier than other recipes so it's filling enough to have alongside a salad for a cold day lunch.

serves 8

¼ cup bacon drippings (from 5 thick-cut slices)

2 tablespoons vegetable oil

2 large eggs

1½ cups whole buttermilk

1 (15.25-ounce) can corn kernels, drained

½ onion, finely chopped (½ cup)

1¼ cups self-rising white cornmeal mix

½ cup self-rising soft-wheat flour (such as White Lily)

¾ cup grated extra-sharp Cheddar cheese (3 ounces)

1. Preheat the oven to 400°F. Place the bacon drippings and vegetable oil in a 10-inch cast-iron skillet; heat in the oven for 4 minutes.

2. Whisk together the egg and buttermilk in a large mixing bowl. Stir in the corn and onion.

3. Whisk together the cornmeal mix and flour in a medium bowl; gently stir into the buttermilk mixture.

4. Remove the hot skillet from the oven; carefully pour half of the hot drippings into the batter. (The drippings will sizzle and sputter.) Whisk to combine. Pour half of the batter into the skillet.

5. Sprinkle half of the cheese evenly over the batter. Pour the remaining half of the batter over the cheese and top with the remaining cheese.

6. Bake at 400°F for 30 to 35 minutes or until golden brown and the cornbread pulls away from sides of the skillet. Let cool 15 minutes before serving.

———◆———

Green Goddess Romaine Salad

Green goddess dressing has always been one of my favorites. I normally make a double batch and use it as a dipping sauce for vegetables. The romaine lettuce can be cut into quarters an hour in advance, covered with a damp paper towel, and refrigerated until serving.

serves 8

1 small garlic clove, peeled

2 anchovies, packed in oil

¼ cup chopped fresh flat-leaf parsley

2 tablespoons chopped fresh chives

1 tablespoon chopped fresh tarragon

Zest of 1 lemon

1 tablespoon Dijon mustard

1 tablespoon white wine vinegar

¼ cup plain Greek yogurt

⅓ cup mayonnaise

¼ teaspoon table salt

⅛ teaspoon freshly ground black pepper

2 romaine hearts

1 pint cherry tomatoes sliced in half, preferably all different colors

1. Pulse the garlic and anchovies in a food processor until finely chopped. Add the parsley and next 9 ingredients, and process until smooth. Chill until serving.

2. Cut the romaine hearts into fourths, lengthwise. Arrange them side by side on a platter. Pour the dressing down the length of each fourth. Top with the tomatoes.

Slow-Cooker Apple Crisp

Having a warm dessert ready in a slow cooker is such a gift to anyone who entertains. Thanks to cinnamon and maple syrup bubbling away, your house smells heavenly when guests arrive. If the crisp is ready before serving time, turn off the slow cooker and just turn it back on low to reheat. I swear by Honey Crisp apples for this recipe, but Pink Ladies and Jonagold varieties also work well.

serves 6 to 8

3½ pounds sweet-tart Honey Crisp apples, peeled and cut into ¼-inch-thick slices

2 tablespoons fresh lemon juice

2 tablespoons pure maple syrup

1 teaspoon vanilla extract

¾ cup all-purpose flour

½ cup firmly packed light brown sugar

1 teaspoon ground cinnamon

⅛ teaspoon allspice

⅛ teaspoon table salt

½ cup cold unsalted butter, cut into ½-inch pieces

¾ cup chopped and toasted pecans

Vanilla Bean Ice Cream, page 219

1. Place the apples in a lightly greased 6-quart slow cooker. Combine lemon juice and next 2 ingredients. Pour over apples and toss to coat.

2. Combine the flour and next 4 ingredients in a medium bowl. Cut the butter into the flour mixture with a pastry blender until the mixture resembles coarse meal; sprinkle over the apples.

3. Cover and cook on HIGH for 2 hours and 30 minutes to 3 hours or until the apples are tender with gently pricked with a fork. Sprinkle with the pecans. Serve warm with ice cream.

Recipe Index

Index

glassware:
  crystal stemware, 130
  for home bar, 114, 115
grapefruit, in Ruby Red
  Ambrosia, 160, 162
Green Beans, Lemon-
  Shallot, 181, 182–83,
  185
Green Goddess Romaine
  Salad, 225, 226–27
greeting guests at door,
  55
grits:
  Cheese, Make-Ahead
    Luxury, 211, 213
  Cream Cheese,
    162–63, 165
guests, 133–39
  alert host of spills, 135
  arrival time of, 135
  children as, 25, 82, 83,
    134, 139
  gifts for, 58
  greeting at door, 55
  hostess gifts and, 13,
    24, 48, 136, 139
  introducing, 58
  parking for, 25, 34,
    135
  RSVPing by, 13, 24,
    134
  rude or tipsy, 58
  staying overnight, 139
  thank-you notes
    from, 17, 24–25,
    139

H
Ham, Rosemary Biscuits
  with Red-Eye Aioli
  and, 148, 150
help from friends, 131
home, party basics for,
  29–38
Horseradish Sauce,
  Creamy, 180, 187
hostess gifts, 13, 24, 48,
  136, 139

I
ice, for drinks, 116

Ice Cream, Vanilla Bean,
  218, 219
introducing guests, 58
invitations, 18, 20–25, 21
  electronic, 23
  information to
  include on, 25, 27, 34,
    48
  RSVPing to, 13, 24,
    134

J
Jam, Fig and Red Onion,
  215
Junior Leagues, 84
Just Chess Pie, 188, 189

K
Kalamata, Cucumber,
  and Tomato Salad,
  172–73, 174
Key Lime Tassies, 175–76,
  177
kitchen:
  cleaning, 30, 131
  guests congregating
    in, 131

L
Lassiter, Debra, 10
Limeade, Tart Cherry,
  203, 206
lipstick stains, 72, 78, 155
Lunch, Garden Club,
  166, 167–76, 172–73

M
Ma'ams and Sirs, 17
manners, see etiquette
menus:
  Bloody Mary Brunch,
    154–65, 162–63
  Bride's New
    Monogram
    Shower, 144,
    145–52, 148–49
  Drinks on the Porch,
    201–9, 202–3
  Funeral Reception,
    179–89, 180–81

Garden Club Lunch,
  166, 167–76,
  172–73
Sunset Summer
  Barbecue,
  210–19, 212–13
Supper Club with
  Friends, 220,
  221–28, 226–27
Tailgate at Home,
  191–98, 192–93
mint julep cups, 46
mixers, 111, 117
Mojitos, Peach, 208, 209
monograms, 72, 73,
  74–75, 145
music, 51

N
napkins, 72, 74–75
  cleaning, 72, 78
  folding, 77
  monograms on, 72,
    73, 74–75
  table manners and,
    80, 135
notes, 13, 17
  thank-you, 17, 24–25,
    139

O
olives:
  Herb and Orange
    Marinated, 203,
    204
  Kalamata, Cucumber,
    and Tomato
    Salad, 172–73,
    174
onion:
  Red, and Fig Jam, 215
  Vidalia, Chimichurri,
    180, 187
open houses, 84
orange(s):
  and Cilantro Slaw,
    212, 214
  Ruby Red Ambrosia,
    160, 162
outdoor entertaining, 40,
  48, 85, 86–87

Favorites

The South is overflowing with creative people that are making food and parties more fun for all of us! I always make it a point to do business as locally as possible and it almost always tastes the best. To list them all would take another book but these are some of my favorites right now:

Nearly every item in my kitchen, from appliances to teaspoons, comes from The Cook's Warehouse in Atlanta. There sell everything and can answer any question tossed their way. **cookswarehouse.com**

Marsh Hen Mill on Edisto Island, South Carolina makes Speckled Grits. These stone ground grits exemplify what real grits should take like. **marshhenmill.com**

Brenda Hill in Atlanta has mastered seasonal preserves and jams with less sugar. Her Ginger Pear Preserves and Blueberry-Lime Jam will stop you in your tracks. **thepassionatepreserver.com**

A sustainable stack of pretty fabric napkins makes me happy. I especially love the bargain bundles of mix and match fabrics from Georgia's Dot & Army. **dotandarmy.com**

A former co-worker of mine, Ana Kelly, raises happy sheep to create wonderful cheeses and caramel sauces. True Ewe Vanilla Bean Caramel will change your life. **dayspringdairy.com**

Beautiful Briny Sea makes brilliant sea salt combinations. The Friends Forever Sea Salt combines granulated honey and salt and makes popcorn completely irresistible. **beautifulbrinysea.com**

There's never a time I don't have pecans in my freezer. Local and fresh Georgia pecans from New Ground Orchards are as beautiful as they are delicious. **newgroundorchards.com**

All picnic and beach coolers should save some room for the little bitty cans of Tip Top Proper Cocktails. The Manhattan is our favorite. **tiptopcocktails.com**

When you don't have time for homemade, Callie's Hot Little Biscuits are insanely good. The country ham biscuits make me swoon. **calliesbiscuits.com**

Quail is a Southern delicacy and Manchester Farms Quail in South Carolina is my go-to for the tasty little birds. The quail knots are a must-try. **manchesterfarms.com**

There are a lot of tools and tricks that claim to make shucking oysters easier and safer. Georgia's White Marsh Island Woodworks is the only source you need. Their Tactical Oyster Shucking Towel is made with Kevlar and is completely stab-proof. **whitemarshislandwoodworks.com**

New Creation Soda Works in Athens, Georgia makes seasonal and bright cocktails unbelievably easy. The Nada-Rita Margarita Mix in Strawberry Habanero is unreal. **newcreationsoda.com**

Author's Letter

Dear Friends,

As a child of the South, I was hardwired to gather in times of celebration, mourning, new beginnings, change of seasons, happiness, and sadness. I was taught that it's good manners to bring hot homemade food to someone in need. You bring the food in, set it on the counter, and visit in the kitchen for a few minutes.

It was a given that at the end of a graveside service, mourners would soothe their sadness with heavy food on fine china in the close company of others. When a friend was having a hard time with anything, we poured the wine and opened the door.

I had taken it all for granted.

Until the coronavirus saturated our lives in almost every single way, I considered entertaining– hosting and attending parties—as a fun and festive distraction to everyday life. As the world hunkered down and stayed home, it became clear where the virus thrived. Parties were no longer merry. They were dangerous.

Before the pandemic, I was spoiled in so many ways. I never had to miss spending time with my friends and family. I never had to explain to my children, over and over, why everyday activities were no longer safe. I didn't think about how the company of others is vital to my happiness. I never had to simply wave at my parents from across the porch to keep them safe. The boundaries that the virus forced us to draw were not natural or normal in any way.

As the invitations start arriving in the mail and doorbells ring once again, may we all remember those who were tragically lost and the countless families who had to mourn alone. Let's become more thoughtful in their memory, be better friends and neighbors, and hold on to those we love with all of our might.

Rebecca Lang

Acknowledgments

In the same way that many of the best parties come together, this book is the result of the talents of a community of extraordinary people.

I came to know the gifts of Southern hospitality from my grandmother, Sarah Dopson, and my childhood neighbor, Becky Rawlins. I only wish I would have paid better attention when I was a child. My grandmother was in her prime before I had the sense to appreciate it. There's not a party I host that I don't think of both of them.

My parents, Mandy and William Dopson, are very willing taste testers, babysitters, and always believed in my culinary path. As a parent myself, I now know their sacrifices on my behalf.

I thank God often that Nathalie Dupree gave me a start when she answered the phone when I was only 21.

My editor, Jono Jarrett, jumped in the driver's seat and I've loved taking the ride with him. He's been a blessing and is now a friend.

To say that every author should have an agent like Carole Bidnick is an understatement. For years I have relied on her to look out for my best interests and she always has.

Rizzoli publishes the most beautiful books and I'm honored to have mine in the mix.

I am convinced that Missie Crawford is the world's finest prop stylist. The hardest thing about working with her was trying not to covet every beautiful item she uses in her work. Kathryn McCrary shared her immense talent behind the lens to bring my words to life.

Food stylist Katelyn Hardwick made what seemed like a million biscuits and worked her magic to make it all look effortless. She is welcome back in my kitchen anytime. During photo days in our home, Laurey Glenn captured the best of us. Kelly Sanders made everyone's lives easier. She always seems to be ahead of what you think you need by five minutes.

Teresa Cole shared her designing skills and love on every page you see. Donna Baldone proofread with a fine-toothed comb.

Kelly Troiano and Anne Cain drank wine with me until we had brainstormed the perfect book title. Through Wendy and Jeff Gleim, I learned the art of catering on a scale that can only be achieved in Charleston, SC.

Adair Lang's illustration dressed up page 83 with the expertise of a professional.

For those in Birmingham that nurtured and loved this project, I am forever grateful: Rachel West, Paden Reich, Melissa Clark, Melissa Brown, Sid Evans, Nellah McGough, and Ivy Odom.

Collecting beautiful props often takes an army: My sister Natalie Schweers Coghill, Catherine Hardman, Evelyn Dukes, Appointments at Five, and Woodland Gardens (for the most beautifully locally grown flowers) all chipped in to make the magic happen.

Erin Kirk performed what I call surgery on the book and helped keep me sane during the procedure.

My three favorite people in the world, Kevin, Camden, and Adair, make my life complete. Each time I write a book, it takes effort by us all. We make a good team.